AMERICAN TRADE ADJUSTMENT:
THE GLOBAL IMPACT

AMERICAN TRADE ADJUSTMENT: THE GLOBAL IMPACT

William R. Cline

92-1336

INSTITUTE FOR INTERNATIONAL ECONOMICS
WASHINGTON, DC
MARCH 1989

William R. Cline is a Senior Fellow at the Institute for International Economics. He was formerly a Senior Fellow at The Brookings Institution; Deputy Director for Development and Trade Research at the US Treasury Department; Ford Foundation Visiting Professor at the Instituto de Planejamento Econômico e Social Aplicado (IPEA) in Brazil; and Assistant Professor at Princeton University.

INSTITUTE FOR INTERNATIONAL ECONOMICS
11 Dupont Circle, NW
Washington, DC 20036
(202) 328-9000 Telex: 261271 IIEUR Fax: (202) 328-5432

C. Fred Bergsten, *Director*
Ann L. Beasley, *Director of Publications*

The Institute for International Economics was created by, and receives substantial support from, the German Marshall Fund of the United States.

The views expressed in this publication are those of the author. This publication is part of the overall program of the Institute, as endorsed by its Board of Directors, but does not necessarily reflect the views of individual members of the Board or the Advisory Committee.

Printed in the United States of America 93 92 91 90 89   5 4 3 2 1
Library of Congress Cataloging-in-Publication Data

Cline, William R.
    American trade adjustment: the global impact / William R. Cline.
    p.   cm.—(Policy analyses in international economics; 26)

    1. United States—Commercial policy. I. Title II. Series.
HF1455.C57   1989
382'.3'0973—dc19   89-2070
                                                                                    CIP

ISBN 0-88132-095-1

Contents

FIGURES

Preface

This volume presents the main results of an extensive study by William Cline of the outlook for the external imbalances of the United States and the world's other leading economies through 1992. It concludes that the progress of 1986–88 in reducing these imbalances is likely to end soon and in fact go into reverse, on the basis of present policies and exchange rates, and that substantial additional policy measures are therefore needed promptly both in the United States and in a number of other countries.

As with several earlier Institute studies, we are releasing our findings in two different formats in an effort to meet the needs of different groups of readers. A full presentation of Dr. Cline's analytical model, data, and simulations to 1992 can be found in a book-length volume, *United States External Adjustment and the World Economy*, to be released shortly. This shorter version, which is also incorporated as the summary first chapter of the larger volume, presents his main analytical conclusions and policy recommendations.

The Institute has published several previous studies on the international imbalances of the major countries and their effects on the world economy. The first was *Deficits and the Dollar: The World Economy At Risk*, by Stephen Marris, originally released in December 1985 and updated in September 1987. Most recently, my own *America in the World Economy: A Strategy for the 1990s*, published in November 1988, draws heavily on the analyses presented here. Also related was a joint effort by 33 economists from 13 countries, released in December 1987, entitled *Resolving the Global Economic Crisis: After Wall Street*. In all these publications, the Institute has attempted to assess the "big picture" of where the world economy is headed and what policy changes may be needed to promote its successful evolution in the future.

The Institute for International Economics is a private nonprofit institution for the study and discussion of international economic policy. Its purpose is to analyze important issues in that area, and to develop and communicate practical new approaches for dealing with them. The Institute is completely nonpartisan.

The Institute was created by a generous commitment of funds from the German Marshall Fund of the United States in 1981 and now receives about 20 percent of its support from that source. In addition, major institutional grants are being received from the Ford Foundation, the William and Flora Hewlett Foundation, and the Alfred P. Sloan Foundation. A number of other foundations and private corporations are contributing to the increasing diversification of the Institute's resources.

The Board of Directors bears overall responsibility for the Institute and gives general guidance and approval to its research program, including identification of topics that are likely to become important to international economic policymakers over the medium run (generally one to three years), and which thus should be addressed by the Institute. The Director, working closely with the staff and outside Advisory Committee, is responsible for the development of particular projects and makes the final decision to publish an individual study.

The Institute hopes that its studies and other activities will contribute to building a strong foundation for international economic policy around the world. We invite readers of these publications to let us know how they think we can best accomplish this objective.

C. FRED BERGSTEN
Director
February 1989

Acknowledgments

The author thanks Paul Armington, C. Fred Bergsten, Bela Balassa, Richard N. Cooper, Anne K. McGuirk, Richard Portes, John Williamson, and Masaru Yoshitomi for insightful comments. He gratefully acknowledges the cooperation of William Helkie and Peter Hooper of the US Federal Reserve Board in the use of their forecasting model. He expresses his great appreciation for the excellent work of research assistants Jonathan Conning, who prepared the data and programming for the multicountry model, and Alex Pfaff and John Hopkins. Andrea Pinkney and Anthony Stancil provided word processing assistance.

This study is dedicated to the author's daughter, Marian.

American Trade Adjustment: The Global Impact

Since the mid-1980s the United States has run huge external deficits, which reached as high as $154 billion on the current account (merchandise trade and services, including capital income) in 1987. Prudence requires that this annual imbalance be cut by at least $100 billion over the next few years. Although the current account deficit did decline to approximately $137 billion in 1988,[1] under present policies it is likely to remain well above $100 billion in 1989 despite further modest reduction, and the deficit is then likely to widen again in 1990 and beyond (as analyzed in this study). Elimination of the US fiscal deficit and some further real decline of the dollar are likely to be required to achieve a sustainable external balance.

The solution of the US external deficit problem, however, could cause new economic difficulties for other countries, many of which relied heavily on exports to the United States to fuel their economic growth earlier in the 1980s. Patterns of major imbalances among other nations persist, as large surpluses remain in Japan and Germany, as well as Taiwan and Korea, while external positions of Third World debtor countries remain weak. In addition, there are rising deficits in the United Kingdom and some other intermediate industrial countries. These emerging weaknesses could intensify once the United States does begin to deal forcefully with its own deficits. In particular, the weaker foreign economies could bear a disproportionately large share of

---

1. The trade deficit on a balance of payments basis stood at $126.5 billion. Based on the nonmerchandise current account in the first three quarters, the full-year current account deficit stood at $136.6 billion. US Department of Commerce, *Merchandise Trade: Fourth Quarter and Year 1988, Balance of Payments Basis* (Washington: US Department of Commerce, BEA 89–06, 28 February 1988), hereafter referred to as *Commerce 1988 Trade;* and US Department of Commerce, *Summary of US International Transactions: Third Quarter 1988,* BEA 88–57 (Washington: US Department of Commerce, 13 December 1988), hereafter referred to as *Commerce 1988:3 Current Account.*

1

the counterpart of falling US external deficits, in the absence of special measures to concentrate the impact on the high-surplus countries.

This study examines what measures will be needed to achieve the required correction in the US external accounts, and goes on to analyze the nature of international adjustment necessary to ensure that correction of the US external deficit can occur smoothly, without provoking new imbalances abroad and risking international recession.

1 Origins and Importance of the External Imbalance

The large US external deficit is the legacy of economic policies adopted in the early 1980s. The central feature of these policies was an unusual combination of fiscal stimulus with monetary restraint. Tax revenues failed to rise as rapidly as many supply-side advocates had hoped after the 1981 tax cut, and the total fiscal deficit (federal, state, and local) rose from 1 percent of GNP in 1981 to an average of 3.4 percent of GNP in 1982–86.[2] This stimulus pulled the economy out of the severe 1982 recession, and permitted the creation of 17 million jobs during the course of the decade. Meanwhile monetary restraint, aided by the good fortune of falling oil prices, made possible a reduction of US inflation from its peak of nearly 14 percent in 1980 to about 4 percent by 1988.

Unfortunately, these gains came only at the expense of the so-called "twin deficits": the internal fiscal deficit and the external deficit on trade and services. The rising fiscal deficit caused a widening gap between the domestic use and availability of resources. Private saving did not rise to offset the decline in public sector saving—on the contrary, gross private saving fell from approximately 18 percent of GNP in 1979–81 to 16 percent in 1985–87, largely because of falling personal savings rates. Instead, foreign resources had to be called upon to fill the resource gap. Nor was the resulting inflow of foreign capital (and the goods and services it financed) dedicated to a boom in US investment, which might have justified borrowing abroad. The ratio of gross private investment to GNP actually declined from 17 percent

---

2. References for these and other data not otherwise cited here are given in my *United States External Adjustment and the World Economy* (Washington: Institute for International Economics, forthcoming).

in 1979–81 to less than 16 percent in 1985–87. The nation had simply gone on a spree of private and government consumption, financed by foreigners.

The resource gap caused high real interest rates, as the government vied with the private sector to borrow in the credit market. High interest rates attracted capital from abroad, and this capital inflow bid up the real price of the dollar by some 40 percent or more. The overvalued dollar acted like a tax of this amount on exports, and a subsidy of the same size to imports. As a result (and because of a higher rate of growth in the United States than abroad, as well as curtailed US exports to the debtor nations following the debt crisis), in the first half of the 1980s the value of US exports stagnated while imports rose by nearly 50 percent despite lower oil prices.

The large US external deficit poses three major risks. The first is that failure of the deficit to show progress toward further reduction could at some point provoke a collapse in foreign confidence in the dollar and in the US economy, causing a sharp decline in the dollar well beyond the moderate further reduction from current levels needed to correct the external deficit. Under these circumstances, US monetary authorities would be likely to permit (or even encourage) a large rise in interest rates to stem the excessive fall of the dollar and its threat to revive inflation. A surge in interest rates by perhaps some 5 percentage points would be likely to lead to domestic recession. There would thus be a "hard landing" for both the dollar and the US economy.[3] There have already been storm warnings that the hard-landing scenario could occur, as two episodes of rising US interest rates in 1987 (when foreign private finance began to dry up and central banks had to finance most of the US external deficit) provoked first a bond market collapse and then the stock market crash of October.

The second risk of a large external deficit is that, if it continues over the longer term, the United States will be forced to maintain high real interest rates indefinitely to attract ongoing financing from abroad. High interest rates would discourage investment and thus limit longer-term economic growth.

---

3. For the first and definitive statement of this risk, see Stephen Marris, *Deficits and the Dollar: The World Economy at Risk.* POLICY ANALYSES IN INTERNATIONAL ECONOMICS 14 (Washington: Institute for International Economics, December 1985). Note that the crucial dynamic of the hard landing is one of "bandwagon" expectations that cause a falling dollar to plunge far below its longer-term equilibrium level. The rise of the dollar in 1988 (after its three-year decline) somewhat reduces this risk by serving notice to speculators that simple extrapolation of past trends can be costly. However, from another standpoint the risk of the hard landing rises while net external debt is rising faster than exports or GNP.

The burden imposed on the next generation would be twofold: not only would Americans have to service a large net external debt (already projected at close to $1 trillion by 1992), but in addition the American economy would have a smaller production base from which to make these payments.[4]

The third risk is an outbreak of protectionism. Congress was already moving toward higher protection in 1985 before the Plaza Agreement among governments to bring the dollar down from its excessively strong levels. If the US trade and current account deficits fail to decline after 1989 and begin to widen again, as projected in this study, there is considerable risk that politicians will conclude that macroeconomic policies such as exchange rate changes have had their chance and failed, and that the time has come to impose direct import restrictions. New protectionist measures and the foreign retaliation they would be likely to incite could only push the world economy toward recession.[5]

2   Medium-Term Prospects for the US External Deficits

Because of the risks of persistent high external deficits, it is crucial to diagnose whether the US trade and current account balances are well on their way toward correction, or whether instead more energetic policy measures are required to achieve adjustment. This study applies two econometric models to project the medium-term path of the US external accounts.

RECENT TRENDS

In 1987 the exchange markets began to despair that the US trade deficit would ever decline. Although the dollar had begun its descent by the second quarter of 1985, the nominal trade deficit for 1987 was larger than ever

---

4. If the external deficit were being used to finance unusually high domestic investment, this concern would not be relevant. However, as noted, the foreign financing has been used for consumption rather than investment.

5. For an overview of these risks and comprehensive policy proposals for correcting the US external deficit, see C. Fred Bergsten, *America in the World Economy: A Strategy for the 1990s* (Washington: Institute for International Economics, 1988).

before at $160 billion versus $122 billion in 1985 and $145 billion in 1986 (see table B-1 of Annex B).[6] Actually the continued widening of the trade deficit should have come as no great surprise, in view of past lags of up to two years in the exchange rate–trade relationship.[7] It takes time for firms to recognize the exchange rate change as permanent and to change their prices accordingly; then, for purchasers to change their buying decisions; and thereafter, for deliveries to arrive following new orders. Only after such lags do the increased volumes of exports and decreased volumes of imports begin to more than offset the initial adverse effect of higher nominal import prices after depreciation (the J-curve phenomenon).

By 1988, enough time had elapsed for trade to respond, and by the first quarter of that year the nominal value of US exports stood fully 32 percent higher than in the same period of 1987 (balance of payments basis), in contrast to their lackluster rise of only 2.3 percent from 1986 to 1987 as a whole. Favorable trade data brought exchange market euphoria, while the Group of Seven (G-7) moved forcefully to support the dollar at the beginning of the year, and the dollar began to rise again.

By late 1988 there were signs that the export boom was beginning to slow down, and progress in reducing the trade deficit appeared even more in jeopardy. Seasonally adjusted exports for the fourth quarter compared with those of the second showed that the annual growth rate had decelerated to 11 percent; and while the average quarterly trade deficit had fallen from $40 billion in 1987 to approximately $30 billion by the second quarter of 1988,

---

6. In real terms the merchandise trade deficit did decline in 1987, from $168.6 billion to $158.9 billion at 1982 prices. However, the rise in dollar import prices meant that the nominal value widened. Note that the trade balance data used here refer to the balance of payments concept, which treats imports on an f.a.s. (free alongside ship) basis and excludes sales by military agencies. Press reports more commonly refer to the trade balance with imports on a c.i.f. (cost including insurance and freight) basis. That deficit stood at $170.3 billion in 1987 and $137.3 billion in 1988. US Department of Commerce, *US Merchandise Trade: December 1988*, FT 900 (Washington: US Department of Commerce).

7. Whether this time there was a "hysteresis" that fundamentally reduced or unusually delayed the trade response to the exchange rate remains a matter of debate. One popular argument has been that foreign firms accepted reduced profit margins rather than raise their dollar prices. However, tests comparing actual dollar export prices to what would have been expected on the basis of foreign wholesale prices divided by dollar exchange rates show an extremely close tracking for the cases of Germany, France, and Italy, with little room for supposed breaks in the exchange rate–export price relationship. Tests for Japan and the United Kingdom show somewhat more evidence of lagging export price adjustment after 1985.

it remained stuck at that plateau through the end of the year.[8] Under these circumstances, the dollar began to weaken again in the fourth quarter of 1988, and its renewed strength in early 1989 came not from favorable trade data but in response to rising US interest rates.

Despite the deceleration of improvement, the full-year results for 1988 were encouraging. On a balance of payments basis, US exports rose by 28.2 percent, imports rose by only 8.9 percent, the trade deficit declined by $33.8 billion (to $126 billion), and the current account deficit declined by an estimated $17 billion (to $137 billion).[9]

MODELING TRADE AND CURRENT ACCOUNTS

The abrupt shift from further deterioration of the US trade balance in 1987 to brisk improvement in early 1988, followed by a seeming halt to the gains by the second half, highlights the risks of simple straight-line projections of current trends as a basis for policy formation. For meaningful analysis of the external sector outlook, especially over a horizon of up to five years, it is necessary to apply an econometric model.

This study uses two such models. The first is an adaptation of the quarterly current account model developed at the Federal Reserve Board by Helkie and Hooper.[10] The second is an original multicountry model that provides a second opinion on the prospects for US external accounts, as well as a basis for analyzing the impact of US external adjustment on major foreign countries and regions. Annex A provides a brief technical description of each model.[11]

The HHC Model—The adapted Helkie–Hooper model (HHC) predicts aggregate US nonoil imports, oil imports, nonagricultural exports, and

---

8. *Commerce 1988 Trade.* The fourth quarter outcome (−$32 billion) was actually slightly worse than that of the third (−$29 billion).

9. Based on full-year trade data in *Commerce 1988 Trade* and current account data for three quarters, *Commerce 1988:3 Current Account.*

10. William L. Helkie and Peter Hooper, "An Empirical Analysis of the External Deficit, 1980–86," in Ralph C. Bryant, Gerald Holtham, and Peter Hooper, eds., *External Deficits and the Dollar: The Pit and the Pendulum* (Washington: Brookings Institution, 1988), 10–56.

11. A complete exposition is given in my *United States External Adjustment and the World Economy* (Washington: Institute for International Economics, forthcoming).

agricultural exports.[12] Export prices are determined by the US wholesale price index with export weights, and by a variable for foreign prices (based on foreign consumer prices divided by exchange rates against the dollar). US export prices rise by about 1 percent when the US export-weighted wholesale price rises by 1 percent, and by 0.2 percent when foreign prices rise by 1 percent. There is thus some feedback from exchange rate changes to US export prices: as the dollar depreciates, part of the benefit to US firms takes the form of higher dollar prices, instead of being completely ''passed through'' to foreign buyers in the form of lower foreign currency prices.

Export volume (nonagricultural) in the HHC model depends on foreign income (with an elasticity, or responsiveness, of 2.2, so that a 1 percent rise in GNP abroad causes a 2.2 percent increase in US exports); on the size of the US capital stock relative to the foreign stock (as a measure of trend capacity); and on the price of US exports relative to foreign consumer prices divided by foreign exchange rates, with price lags stretching over two years. Dollar export value equals the quantity of exports multiplied by the price.

Prices of nonoil imports depend on foreign consumer prices, on foreign exchange rates against the dollar (with lags over seven quarters), and on an index of commodity prices. The elasticity of import prices with respect to foreign prices is almost unity, as is the elasticity with respect to the exchange rate, so that the pass-through of foreign price and exchange rate movements over time is nearly total. The volume of nonoil imports depends on capacity utilization in foreign industrial countries, on US income (with a total two-year elasticity of approximately 2), on relative capital stock, and on the ratio of import prices to the US GDP deflator (with lags over seven quarters). The price elasticity is minus 1.15. Since it is close to unity, this elasticity means that nominal import values remain relatively unchanged in response to exchange rate changes, because quantity changes are approximately offset by dollar price changes in the opposite direction.

The HHC model also encompasses services, transfers, and the current account. Capital services play an important role. They are separated into earnings on direct investment, private portfolio holdings, and government obligations. Rates of return depend on interest rates, and the exchange rate has an important valuation effect on direct investment: depreciation of the dollar contributes to higher earnings on assets held abroad by American firms

---

12. The reader not interested in the analytical structure of the models may wish to skip this section and the next.

by virtue of a markup in their dollar value. In general, the capital services segment of the model shows a comparative advantage for the United States in international financial intermediation, as rates of return on US assets abroad tend to exceed those on US liabilities to foreigners. The model also cumulates the current account so that net foreign liabilities build over time as the US remains in deficit, in turn causing the capital services account to deteriorate.

For purposes of this study, two adaptations have been made in the original Helkie–Hooper model. The first is to streamline the model from 431 equations to 130, to facilitate simulation. Numerous equations concerning oil imports and agricultural exports are replaced by simplified projections for these sectors. Agricultural exports are projected to grow by 3 percent annually in volume and by 4 percent in nominal dollar prices. World oil prices are projected on the basis of the "low price" scenario estimated by the National Petroleum Council (NPC), and rise from approximately $15 per barrel in 1988 to nearly $19 in 1992. The NPC baseline volume of US oil imports rises from 7.2 million barrels per day in 1988 to an estimated 10.4 million bpd by 1992. For changes from this baseline caused by changes in US growth, an income elasticity of unity is applied, reflecting a lower income elasticity of demand combined with a stagnant volume of domestic production, so that incremental consumption comes entirely from imports. In the baseline projections, US oil imports rise from $39 billion in 1988 to $72 billion in 1992 (table B-1), and thus grow in value terms at approximately twice the rate of nonoil imports (table B-1).

The second adaptation addresses overprediction of trade prices in the original model, which called for 1987 dollar import prices to stand 14.7 percent higher than the levels that actually occurred, and overpredicted dollar export prices by 7.1 percent. Much of the divergence was attributable to the unusual lag of foreign wholesale prices behind consumer prices in 1986–87 (reflecting lower oil prices) and the model's use of the latter. The adjustment in the HHC model assumes that half of the gap between predicted and actual trade prices by 1987:4 is never closed, but that trade prices catch up to close the other half of the gap over a period of four quarters.

The EAG Model—Whereas the Helkie–Hooper model is among the more prominent of several models of the US external accounts, there are few existing models that provide trade and current account projections for major foreign countries and regions, or permit examination of the impact of US external adjustment on the economies of other countries. The External Adjustment with Growth (EAG) model divides the world into a total of 17 countries and multicountry groupings: the seven largest industrial countries individually; a group of Other Industrial countries; OPEC; Taiwan; Korea, Singapore, and Hong Kong; Argentina; Brazil; Mexico; a group of Other Latin American countries (i.e., excluding those in OPEC); a group of Other African countries; and a Rest of World grouping. All of world trade is incorporated in one or another of the cells of this 17 × 17 matrix, as shown for 1987 in table B-3 (Annex B). Trade is defined as exports from one partner to another; imports are merely the partner's exports to the country in question.

The model separates oil trade implicitly. By identifying OPEC individually it isolates much of oil trade. In addition, the model divides the exports of Mexico and United Kingdom into oil and nonoil.

For each cell in the trade matrix (for example, US exports to Germany), there is a trade equation. This equation relates the real volume of trade to income in the importing area, the direct prices of the exporter relative to domestic prices in the importing area, and the cross-price competition of the exporter in question against all other exporters participating in the market of the importing area in question. Quarterly data for the period 1973–87, drawn from the International Monetary Fund's (IMF) *Direction of Trade Statistics,* are used to estimate the trade equations. Prices are the IMF's unit value export prices (which are uniform for a given exporting country or group in its trade with all of the other countries or groups). The domestic price term for the importing country is the country's wholesale price index divided by its exchange rate against the dollar. The estimation procedure sets upper and lower bounds on the acceptable elasticities (3.0 and 0.3, respectively, in absolute value). It applies nonlinear programming to minimize the sum of squared residuals in obtaining the estimates, subject to these constraints.

For oil trade, the price of oil is projected independently as discussed above. Oil import volumes depend on income growth in the importing area, with an income elasticity of 0.5 (except for the United States, where the elasticity is set at 1.0 as discussed above).

Imports of OPEC depart from the general model. They are determined by applying a fixed respending ratio out of export earnings, and distributing total imports across supplier countries according to past averages.

The EAG model includes a simple current account estimation for each country. Nonfactor services, such as shipping and insurance, are set proportional to merchandise trade (on both the import and export sides) in the base year 1987. Capital services are based on an "inherited" component reflecting the rate of net capital earnings in the base year, and an incremental component capturing the earnings on the cumulative current account balance over the period 1988–92.

Table A-3 of Annex A provides a summary view of the elasticities estimated in the EAG model. In general the elasticities are relatively high. The responsiveness to price is sufficient to meet the Marshall–Lerner conditions for exchange rate depreciation to improve the trade balance: the sum of the price elasticities, in absolute value, is greater than unity. Import income elasticities have a trade-weighted average of approximately 2.0. For some countries (United States, United Kingdom, France, Canada, and Argentina), the income elasticity for imports exceeds that for exports,[13] whereas for others (Japan, Brazil, Mexico, Taiwan, Korea–Singapore–Hong Kong) the reverse is true. Such divergences imply a tendency for the trade balance to deteriorate or improve over time, respectively.

EAG Backcasts and Model Adjustments—Table B-3 shows the 1987 trade matrix for the countries and groups identified in the EAG model. The table shows the dominant role of the United States, Germany, Japan, and the blocs Other Industrial and Rest of World in total world trade. It also shows the large trade deficit of the United States and the large surpluses of Japan and Germany in the base year.

Figure A-1 compares actual total imports and exports for the United States, Germany, and Japan (the three largest trading countries) from 1975 through 1987 with the levels predicted or "backcast" from the EAG model. It also shows EAG-predicted and actual bilateral trade between the United States and Canada, Japan, and Germany. As the figure indicates, the model achieves a close fit with actual trade in the past. There is, nonetheless, a tendency for the model to underpredict US imports in 1987, and correspondingly to underpredict exports of Japan and certain other key countries (such as Taiwan) to the United States in that year. The impact of the 1986 decline in the dollar on 1987 US imports was less than predicted by the model for trade with some important countries.

To address these divergences and more generally to ensure that prediction

---

13. This is the so-called "Houthakker-Magee" phenomenon identified for the United States in the late 1960s. Hendrik S. Houthakker and Stephen P. Magee, "Income and Price Elasticities in World Trade," *Review of Economics and Statistics*, 51, no. 2, May 1969.

errors in the important 1987 base year do not distort the medium-term forecasts, for projection purposes the EAG model is recalibrated to place estimated 1987 trade halfway between the actual levels and those predicted by the unadjusted model. In addition, to reduce the vulnerability of the projections to idiosyncrasies in the estimated elasticities for individual trade equations, the projection model applies in each case an average between the estimated specific elasticity and a "uniform" elasticity for the entire model, which in turn is equal to the trade-weighted average value for the elasticity in question (table A-1).[14] A further adjustment imposes a consistency constraint across the substitution elasticities for the class of countries whose currencies are expected to appreciate in exchange rate simulations and all others, so that changes in US trade from the first group must offset changes from the second insofar as the substitution effect is concerned.

BASELINE PROJECTIONS

The base case economic assumptions are as follows. The United States is assumed to make little if any further progress in reducing its fiscal deficit.[15] The dollar is projected to remain constant at its real level against other currencies of the fourth quarter of 1987. The dollar had returned to approximately this level by early 1989, and its rise in 1988 through August is likely to have been regarded by firms as transitory. Average real GNP growth in 1989–92 is placed at 2.6 percent annually for the United States and Canada, 2.5 percent for Europe, 4 percent for Japan, 8 percent for Taiwan and Korea, and 4½ percent in the rest of the world. World inflation is assumed to average 4½ percent annually in dollar terms.

---

14. A high estimated price elasticity for US exports to Canada in particular places a disproportionately large share of future US adjustment on trade with that country; dilution by averaging with the uniform elasticities yields more plausible results.

15. This assumption follows the Congressional Budget Office projections that the federal fiscal deficit, which stood at $155 billion in fiscal 1988, will be $155 billion in 1989, $141 billion in 1990, $140 billion in 1991, and $135 billion in 1992 (fiscal years). Although these forecasts nonetheless reflect a reduction in the deficit relative to GNP, from 3.2 percent in FY1988 to 2.2 percent in FY1992, they may be too optimistic, as they are based on "current services" and do not allow for likely program expansions. Congressional Budget Office, *The Economic and Budget Outlook: Fiscal Years 1990–1994* (Washington: Congressional Budget Office, January 1989), xv.

TABLE 1   **US trade projections, 1987–92** (billions of current dollars)[a]

	1987	1988	1989	1990	1991	1992
Exports						
EAG	252.6	304.7	359.1	402.8	449.1	500.9
EAG-BOP	251.7	303.7	357.9	401.5	447.6	499.3
HHC	249.6	339.0	404.2	445.8	496.1	553.6
Average	250.6	321.4	381.0	423.6	471.8	526.4
Imports						
EAG	389.3	423.3	461.4	511.0	565.0	624.7
EAG-BOP	393.7	428.1	466.7	516.9	571.5	631.8
HHC	409.8	466.9	505.1	553.2	611.7	670.1
Average	401.8	447.5	485.9	535.0	591.6	651.0
Trade balance						
EAG	−136.7	−118.5	−102.4	−108.2	−115.9	−123.7
EAG-BOP	−142.0	−124.4	−108.8	−115.4	−123.9	−132.6
HHC	−160.2	−127.9	−100.9	−107.4	−115.7	−116.4
Average	−151.1	−126.2	−104.8	−111.4	−119.8	−124.5
Current account balance						
EAG	−152.6	−136.6	−122.2	−134.7	−150.7	−168.0
HHC	−153.9	−138.2	−114.9	−124.4	−135.6	−138.4
Average	−153.2	−137.4	-118.6	−129.6	−143.2	−153.2
Current account balance as % of XGS						
EAG	−47	−35	−27	−26	−26	−26
HHC	−36	−27	−19	−19	−19	−18
Average	−48	−34	−25	−25	−24	−24

a. Projections are at real exchange rates of 1987:4.
EAG-BOP = on balance of payments basis using the EAG model; XGS = exports of goods and nonfactor services. EAG and HHC are alternative projection models (see text).

Table B-1 shows the baseline projections of the US trade and current accounts using the HHC model. Table B-4 shows the corresponding world trade matrix projected for 1992 using the EAG model. Table 1 presents the summary projections of the two models, and figure 1 illustrates their projections for the trade and current account balances.

The model projections are from a 1987 base, and comparison of projected

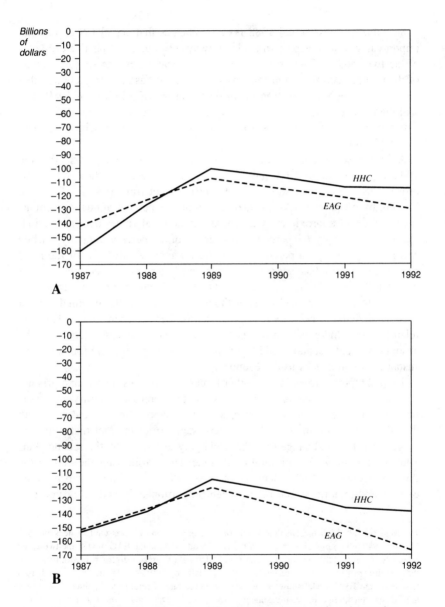

FIGURE 1:   Projections of baseline US external accounts using alternative
models. A: Trade balance; B: current account balance.

1988 values against actual 1988 results indicates that actual US export and import values both lie approximately halfway between the respective estimates of the two models. The best estimate thus appears to be the simple average of the two projections.[16] On this basis, the central baseline projection is that the US trade deficit will drop no further than to $105 billion in 1989, and will then rise again to $125 billion by 1992. The current account deficit will similarly reach a trough of $119 billion in 1989, and then widen again to over $150 billion by 1992.

As indicated in table 1, the nominal values of trade rise briskly through 1992, especially in the HHC model. Based on the average of the two models' projections, US exports should rise by 110 percent from 1987 to 1992, and imports by 62 percent. As world inflation at 4½ percent annually accounts for increases of approximately 25 percent in nominal values over the period, real exports rise by 68 percent (an average of 11 percent annually), while real imports rise by 30 percent (5½ percent annually). Because of the rapid rise of the export base (especially in nominal terms), the current account deficit falls from 48 percent of exports of goods and nonfactor services in 1987 to 24 percent by 1992, even though by that year the nominal current account deficit is once again back up to the $150 billion range. Thus, in relative terms there is improvement even in the base case. Even so, the absolute current account deficit remains far too large for comfort about its sustainability and risks to the economy.

Table 2 reports projections of other forecasting entities, public and private. It is evident from the table that most of the forecasts identify the same inverse-U profile for the US current account balance that is found with both the HHC and EAG models. This pattern stems from the fact that, with the lagged effects of exchange rate change largely exhausted by the second year, 1989 should show the minimum US trade deficit following the end to the dollar's decline in 1987. Because there is still a $100 billion gap between exports and imports at that point, when proportionate growth in response to

---

16. Note that although the absolute levels of both imports and exports tend to lie some $35 billion to $40 billion higher each year in the HHC model than in the EAG model, the two agree relatively closely on the size of the trade deficit. They show greater divergence with respect to the magnitude of the current account deficit, especially by 1991–92. As may be derived from table B-1, the HHC model shows a persistently higher rate of return on US direct investment abroad than on foreign direct investment in the United States, and from this standpoint may introduce an upward bias of perhaps some $15 billion annually by 1991 in the current account estimate.

TABLE 2   **Alternative projections of the US current account balance** (billions of current dollars)

Study	Date	Real exchange rate basis	Projections				
			1988	1989	1990	1991	1992
IMF	October 1988	August 1988	-129	-129			
OECD	December 1988	November 2, 1988	-132	-116	-108		
DRI–Gault	December 1987	July 1988					
Excluding trend term[a]			-137	-134	-154	-177	-201
Including trend term			-133	-138	-169	-204	-243
DRI–business	October 1988	Rate not fixed	-134	-126	-96	-83	-92
WEFA	September 1988	Rate not fixed	-143	-137	-138	-156	-161
Bryant	January 1988	December 22, 1987	-125	-108	-113	-127	
Cline (HHC–EAG average)	November 1988	1987:4	-137	-119	-130	-143	-153

a. The DRI forecasts are made with and without a term to incorporate the past adverse trend in the current account.

Sources: International Monetary Fund (IMF), *World Economic Outlook,* October 1988, 92; Organization for Economic Cooperation and Development, *OECD Economic Outlook,* December 1988, 71; Nigel Gault, "The Outlook for the US Current Account Deficit," Testimony before the Joint Economic Committee, US Congress, September 13, 1988, and by communication; Ralph C. Bryant, "The US External Deficit: An Update," *Brookings Discussion Papers in International Economics 63,* January 1988, Table 3; WEFA Group, *US Macro Model: Medium-Term Forecast* (Bala Cynwyd, Penn.: WEFA 1988); DRI, *International Business and Financial Outlook: Third Quarter 1988* (Lexington, Mass: DRI 1988:3), 42.

domestic and foreign income growth resumes, the absolute size of the trade deficit begins to widen again. World inflation at 4½ percent annually (in dollar terms) also causes the nominal deficit to swell after 1989. For the current account deficit, the renewed widening is augmented by the growing burden of interest payments on rising net external liabilities. As indicated in table B-1, net US external liabilities reach $1.1 trillion by 1992 in the base case.

Overall, the baseline projections of the HHC and EAG models, and of several other private and official organizations, indicate that in the absence of policy change the US trade and current account deficits will not fall below $100 billion and will begin to increase again after 1989. The policy implication of these projections is that far more needs to be done to reduce the US external deficits to sustainable levels that can forestall the economic and protectionist risks outlined above.

In late 1988, the US Treasury issued a report challenging the conventional models that show results such as those summarized here. The Treasury authors argued that, because of fundamental changes US industry has made in recent years to cut costs and improve quality, there would be a more positive response of US exports than standard models predict from past experience. They added that the increased presence of foreign investment should mean a partial replacement of imports by goods produced by foreign firms in the United States.[17]

It is unclear what basis the Treasury had in mind for anticipating a stronger response of exports than predicted by models estimated from past performance. Although it is true that US labor costs have fallen sharply relative to those of competing nations, this improvement should already be taken into account in the relative price terms of the models.[18] As for direct investment effects,

---

17. US Department of Treasury, *Report to Congress on International Economic and Exchange Rate Policy* (Washington: Treasury Department, 15 October 1988). The report also stated that the Group of Seven countries stood ready to adjust policies to ensure reduction of trade imbalances, but the baseline projections here assume no policy change so that the needed scope of policy adjustment can be analyzed.

18. In a rare attempt to quantify these effects, Hooper has examined indicators of absolute unit labor costs and found that the higher competitive position of US manufacturing by late 1987 might yield a higher trade balance than predicted by the conventional models, by as much as nearly $60 billion by 1993. This outcome would still leave the current deficit at a plateau of approximately $100 billion. However, Hooper's estimate of these supply-side effects has an extremely wide variance. Moreover, in subsequent work Hooper raises new doubts about the

the most important sector is automobiles. There, the presence of voluntary export restraints in Japan meant the existence of an economic rent that could be reduced without necessarily changing the volume of Japanese exports to the United States, so that new "transplant" autos could replace primarily US production rather than imported cars from Japan. Moreover, the transplant firms have a high import content, and their expansion may be expected to increase imports of components.[19] For policy purposes it would thus appear dangerous to take a complacent attitude about large projected external deficits on grounds that effects absent in the models will provide a major improvement.

3 Distortions in International Payments

The baseline projections in the EAG model reveal important distortions in the medium-term outlook for international payments balances that go well beyond an excessive US deficit. The counterpart of this deficit is not distributed evenly. Instead, the foreign surpluses are highly concentrated in Japan and Germany. The pattern of 1992 trade balances bears a close resemblance to the existing structure of high concentrations of surpluses in these countries. Moreover, the absolute size of these surpluses rises over time in the base case, reaching $136 billion in Japan and $85 billion in Germany by 1992 (table 3).

At least four adjustment problems emerge from the baseline projections. The first is the need for the United States to reduce its prospective external deficit. The second is the need for Germany and Japan to reduce their exceptionally large surpluses. Third, the United Kingdom faces a large prospective external deficit. Fourth, some of the intermediate industrial countries face emerging external deficit problems, in considerable measure as the counterpart of the rising German surplus. Surprising weaknesses

---

prospects for such effects, particularly in light of the strengthening of investment growth in Europe and slackening of that in the United States. Peter Hooper, "Exchange Rates and US External Adjustment in the Short Run and the Long Run," *Brookings Discussion Papers in International Economics* 65 (Washington: Brookings Institution, October 1988); also William L. Helkie and Peter Hooper, "U.S. External Adjustment: Progress and Prospects" (Washington: Federal Reserve Board, February 1989).

19. W.V. Bussmann, "The Trade Deficit in Autos with Japan: How Much Improvement?" *Business Economics,* April 1988, 20–25.

develop, not only for the United Kingdom but also, to a lesser degree, for France, Italy, and the Other Industrial countries. Moreover, these weaknesses emerge even in the absence of US external adjustment. If the United States were to achieve a major reduction in its external deficit in the absence of other measures to affect the developing distribution of trade and payments balances among other nations, the potential difficulties faced by the weaker industrial countries would be intensified.

Table 3 provides a summary view of the trends in external accounts for each of the 17 major countries and country groupings examined in the EAG model. The table reports actual 1987 and projected 1992 trade and current account balances. The 1992 estimates include not only the base case discussed above, but also a Feasible Adjustment Package (FAP) case, developed below. Table B-4 shows the projected baseline trade matrix for 1992, and thus indicates the detailed composition of the trade balances that lie behind the summary in table 3. Table 4 summarizes the corresponding bilateral US trade positions, and indicates the persistence of large US bilateral deficits with Japan, Germany, and the East Asian NICs in the base case of no policy change. It is evident from the tables that the major trading nations and groupings divide into several distinct tiers with respect to the medium-term strength of their external accounts.

GERMANY AND JAPAN

In the strongest tier, Germany and Japan further increase their already large external surpluses. Thus, Germany's trade surplus rises from $70 billion to approximately $90 billion, while that of Japan increases from $96 billion to $129 billion in the base case with no additional policy adjustment. The bilateral US deficit with Japan reaches $60 billion by 1992, threatening intensified pressure for protection against imports from that country. The corresponding current account surpluses rise from $45 billion to $85 billion in Germany, and from $87 billion to $136 billion in Japan. Even so, because of a rising nominal export base, the current account surpluses of Germany and Japan are more stable in relative terms, as the German surplus edges up from 14 percent of exports of goods and nonfactor services in 1987 to 16 percent in 1992, while that of Japan remains constant at 34 percent.

The rising absolute surpluses of the two countries may be illustrated as follows. In both, the trade balance remains in strong surplus by 1989. Thus,

TABLE 3 **Trends in trade and current account balances, 1987–92** (billions of dollars except as noted)

Country/group	Trade balance			Current account			Current account as % of XGS		
	1987	1992 Base case	FAP	1987	1992 Base case	FAP	1987	1992 Base case	FAP
United States	-160.2	-124.5	-44.3	-153.9	-153.2	-48.4	-48	-24	-6
United Kingdom	-16.4	-70.8	-32.7	-3.4	-76.1	-22.5	-2	-29	-7
France	-7.5	-16.4	-13.0	-1.5	-6.7	0.4	-1	-2	0
Germany	70.2	89.8	41.0	45.2	84.8	15.7	14	16	3
Italy	-0.5	-14.2	-4.2	-0.7	-20.9	-6.3	0	-9	-2
Canada	8.8	13.7	12.5	-6.3	-11.8	-14.2	-6	-6	-7
Japan	96.4	129.3	80.8	86.6	136.4	63.4	34	34	16
Argentina	1.0	3.8	4.8	-3.7	-3.5	-2.3	-51	-22	-13
Brazil	11.2	26.7	30.1	1.2	15.5	19.1	4	28	31
Mexico	9.6	11.9	12.9	3.9	3.9	5.0	14	9	10
Taiwan	20.7	6.2	1.9	18.0	-1.6	-9.3	32	-2	-11
OPEC	36.0	25.6	25.9	-5.0	-34.8	-34.9	-4	-24	-24
Other Industrial	-8.9	-22.7	-69.1	-6.2	-22.9	-83.1	-1	-2	-8
Korea–Singapore–Hong Kong	6.5	-18.4	-36.8	11.0	-6.9	-27.5	8	-3	-10
Other Latin America	-1.7	4.1	9.2	-9.1	-8.3	-2.0	-30	-14	-3
Other Africa	4.7	1.4	10.5	-4.7	-20.5	-10.2	-8	-21	-9
Rest of World	-37.5	4.5	21.8	-8.0	63.5	89.2	-3	13	16

FAP = Feasible Adjustment Package.
XGS = exports of goods and nonfactor services.

TABLE 4   **Trends in US bilateral trade balances, 1987–92** (billions of dollars)

Bilateral US trade balance	1987	1992 Base case	FAP
United Kingdom	−4.1	3.9	3.9
France	−2.5	−1.7	−0.5
Germany	−16.1	−22.0	−17.1
Italy	−5.6	−6.8	−6.2
Canada	−13.4	−10.8	−1.9
Japan	−56.8	−60.5	−30.0
Argentina	0.1	0.4	0.6
Brazil	−3.6	−8.1	−7.8
Mexico	−4.1	−0.6	0.3
Taiwan	−17.2	−10.1	−3.2
OPEC	−11.4	−16.6	−16.4
Other Industrial	2.2	24.3	39.7
Korea–Singapore–Hong Kong	−22.8	−28.0	−14.5
Other Latin America	0.0	1.8	2.2
Other Africa	−1.3	0.4	1.2
Rest of World	1.6	10.8	14.4

Source: tables B-1 to B-3.
Note: these data are from the EAG data base, and contain minor differences from the data converted to a balance of payments trade data basis (as in table 3).

Japan's exports for this year are estimated at $234 billion, while its imports are projected at $138 billion (EAG model). With lagged effects of the dollar's decline through 1987 broadly exhausted in 1989, thereafter normal import and export growth resumes. Annual dollar inflation contributes 4½ percent each year, and if export and import volumes both rose at 6 percent, nominal trade values would rise by some 30 percent from 1989 to 1992. The large 1989 gap between exports and imports means that in this simple example the proportionate rise boosts Japan's trade surplus to $125 billion by 1992 (the actual model estimate is $129 billion; table 3). In addition, the growing surplus on capital income (from rising net external assets) swamps Japan's traditional deficit on nonfactor services, and adds several billion dollars more to the 1992 current account surplus.

EAST ASIAN NICS

Although the newly industrializing countries (NICs) of East Asia, Taiwan and Korea–Singapore–Hong Kong, are a second strong tier with high current account surpluses in the base year ($18 billion, or 32 percent of exports of goods and services, and $11 billion, or 8 percent, respectively), the two areas show a rapid decline in their surpluses over the five-year period even in the base case without policy adjustment (and at 1987:4 real exchange rates). Thus, Taiwan's current account falls to a deficit equal to 2 percent of exports of goods and services by 1992, while that of Korea–Singapore–Hong Kong turns to a deficit of 3 percent.

For these two areas, the standardized adjustments used in the EAG forecasting model probably introduce a downward bias in future trade and current account balances. In the past the two areas have enjoyed a strong positive difference between the income elasticity of demand for their exports and that for their imports. Thus, for both Taiwan and Korea–Singapore– Hong Kong, the import elasticity is approximately 1.3 whereas the export elasticity is twice as large at 2.7 (table A-3). Such a divergence is typical for high-growth countries, which otherwise would tend to require persistent real depreciation to avoid rising trade imbalances.[20]

The EAG forecasting model dilutes this favorable elasticity asymmetry by averaging the country-specific elasticities with uniform elasticities for all countries on a trade-weighted basis (as discussed above). Although this technique appears to provide more stable projections for the key case of the United States (and especially Canada), it may bias the Taiwan and Korea– Singapore–Hong Kong projections downward by failing to allow sufficient income elasticity asymmetry in view of their growth rates (8 percent annually), which are much higher than the average for other countries (some 3 percent).[21] Nonetheless, the projections do suggest that, if the two areas maintain exceptionally high growth rates, their high external surpluses could well

---

20. For recent empirical documentation of this international pattern, see Paul Krugman, "Differences in Income Elasticities and Trends in Real Exchange Rates," NBER Working Paper No. 2761 (Cambridge, Mass.: National Bureau of Economic Research, 1988).

21. Thus, when country-specific elasticities are applied, the baseline trade balance for Korea– Singapore–Hong Kong in 1992 stands at a surplus of $20 billion rather than a deficit of $11 billion. For Taiwan, the corresponding divergence is between a surplus of $5.3 billion and one of $1.4 billion. The potential bias from averaging country-specific and uniform elasticities thus appears considerably smaller for Taiwan.

diminish substantially over the medium term even without specific policy action.

INTERMEDIATE INDUSTRIAL COUNTRIES

In contrast to the strong baseline trends for external balances in Germany and Japan, the trends are weaker for a tier of intermediate industrial countries. The current account balance declines[22] from − 1 percent of exports of goods and services in 1987 to − 2 percent by 1992 for France, from 0 percent to − 9 percent for Italy, and from − 1 percent to − 2 percent for the Other Industrial countries; it remains at a relatively weak − 6 percent in Canada.[23] In absolute terms the corresponding current account balances all show widening deficits, with 1992 deficits of approximately $21 billion in Italy, $12 billion in Canada, $7 billion in France, and $23 billion in the Other Industrial countries.[24]

Comparison of tables B-3 and B-4 shows that much of this prospective weakness is associated with widening trade imbalances with Germany. Thus, the bilateral trade deficit of France with Germany rises from approximately $12 billion in 1987 to $20 billion by 1992; that of Italy with Germany from $4 billion to $6 billion; and that of the Other Industrial countries with Germany from $31 billion to $38 billion.[25]

UNITED KINGDOM

The weakest external sector outlook is for the United Kingdom, which stands in a class by itself. In the absence of special policy adjustments, the country's

---

22. All references to changing positions on trade or current account "balances" are used in an algebraic sense. An increase in the balance refers to a rise in a surplus or a decline in a deficit. A decline in a balance indicates a reduction in a surplus or an increase in a deficit.

23. For Canada the model actually shows a declining trend, because it substantially overpredicts the level of the current account balance (at zero) in the base year 1987.

24. Note that the Other Industrial country grouping, which includes Australia, Austria, Belgium, Denmark, Finland, Iceland, Ireland, the Netherlands, New Zealand, Norway, Spain, Sweden, and Switzerland, accounts for a large bloc of international trade. Its exports and imports of nearly $500 billion each exceed those of the United States and especially, Germany or Japan.

25. In contrast, bilateral trade with Japan contributes practically nothing to the external sector erosion for France and Italy, although its contribution is comparable to that from trade with Germany in the case of the Other Industrial countries.

current account deficit rises from $3 billion in 1987 to $76 billion in 1992, or from 2 percent of exports of goods and services to 29 percent. Several factors contribute to this outcome. The country has a relatively large adverse asymmetry between income elasticities for exports and imports (even after dilution by averaging with uniform elasticities). Oil accounts for 10 percent of its exports, and oil exports grow slowly in value terms. The United Kingdom has already entered a new cycle of declining external accounts, as the trade balance shifted from surplus in 1980–82 of approximately 7 percent of merchandise exports to deficits of 2.6 percent in 1983–85 and 9.5 percent in 1987. Even if the average percentage changes in imports and exports for other European countries from 1987 to 1992 are applied to the 1987 UK trade base, the adverse initial gap is such that the 1992 trade deficit reaches $31 billion. In addition, UK export prices in dollar terms have risen relatively rapidly since 1986.

OTHER COUNTRIES

Among the other country groupings, there is notable strength in the baseline trend for the Rest of World group, which includes Asia apart from Japan and the NICs (and thus incorporates such countries as China and India); the middle-income countries of Europe (such as Turkey and Portugal); the non-oil-producing nations of the Middle East; and the Eastern bloc countries. Many countries in this area have held real exchange rates against the dollar relatively constant since 1985, and have thus depreciated in real terms against high-income Europe and Japan.[26] The trends are even stronger for Brazil, although that country's unusually low income elasticity for imports probably

---

26. The baseline projection shows the Rest of World current account rising from a deficit of $8 billion in 1987 to a surplus of $63.5 billion in 1992. If it is assumed instead that this developing region spends the potential surplus on increased imports, and that its 1992 baseline current account balance is held to zero, then on the basis of 1992 supplier shares in Rest of World imports (excluding those from other Rest of World countries) the impact would be an increase of current account positions by approximately $7 billion each for the United States, Germany, and Japan; by $9 billion for Korea–Singapore–Hong Kong; and by $12 billion for the Other Industrial countries. This reallocation does not alter the qualitative conclusions of the analysis, as the reduction in the US external deficit is modest and smaller in proportional terms than the corresponding increase in the external surpluses of Germany and Japan.

causes an upward bias in the trend for the trade surplus. Mexico shows moderate external strength but a declining trend.

The levels of current account balances relative to exports, or their baseline trends, or both, tend to be weak for the other groups in the model: Argentina (in the extreme), OPEC, Other Latin America, and Other Africa. These countries are in no position to absorb any of the counterpart of a potential adjustment of the US external deficit.

EARLY EVIDENCE

The EAG model projections use 1987, the most recent year for which data are available for detailed intercountry trade flows, as the base year. The estimates for 1988 are thus projections rather than historical data. By early 1989, initial data on aggregate trade and current account balances for 1988 were becoming available, and they provide a basis for early evidence on the validity of the baseline trends identified in the model.

Salient trends in the baseline projections include persistence and widening of the large surpluses in Germany and Japan, and a large emerging deficit in the United Kingdom. In 1988, Germany's actual trade surplus rose from $70 billion to $79.5 billion, and its current account surplus rose modestly from $45 billion to $49.1 billion.[27] These surpluses are actually larger than the 1988 estimates in the EAG model ($68 billion and $39 billion, respectively), suggesting that the future projections do not exaggerate the surpluses. In Japan, the trade surplus was almost unchanged in 1988 (at an estimated $93 billion versus $96 billion in 1987), whereas the current account surplus declined only modestly (from $87 billion to $79 billion).[28] The EAG projections for 1988 called for a trade surplus of $93 billion and a current account balance of $86 billion, suggesting that the future projections are on track for trade but may be modestly too high for the current account surplus. In the United Kingdom, the deterioration identified in the EAG model was already apparent in 1988, as the trade deficit rose from $17 billion to an estimated $33 billion and the current account deficit from $4 billion to $23 billion (in part because of a cyclical boom in private domestic demand). The

---

27. International Monetary Fund, by communication.
28. The 1987 and estimated 1988 results are from *OECD Economic Outlook*, December 1988.

EAG projections for 1988 were actually more modest: a trade deficit of $25 billion and a current account deficit of $20 billion.

4   The Impact of Policy Measures

The severe distortions in international payments in the baseline projections indicate the need for decisive policy adjustment to reduce international imbalances over the medium term. The key measures for the United States are reduction of the fiscal deficit and some further depreciation of the dollar in real terms. The adjustment measures needed abroad, especially in the high-surplus countries, are the expansion of domestic demand and real exchange rate appreciation.

THE ROLE OF FISCAL ADJUSTMENT AND EXCHANGE RATE CHANGE

The root causes of the US external imbalance are the rise in the fiscal deficit and erosion of personal saving, as discussed above. The first and foremost corrective policy should be full achievement of the Gramm–Rudman–Hollings targets, which would result in elimination of the federal deficit by 1993.[29] Under this act the deficit would be cut by approximately $40 billion annually in each of the next four years.[30]

The national accounts identities (and the resource balance discussed above) establish a direct accounting relationship between the fiscal deficit and the external deficit.[31] It is unlikely, however, that elimination of a fiscal deficit

---

29. If policy instruments existed that could reliably raise personal savings rates, they too would be appropriate. Unfortunately, experience has shown savings rates to be stubbornly resistant to policy measures, including such instruments as Individual Retirement Accounts.

30. The revised act of 1987 sets the following deficit targets: fiscal 1988, $144 billion; 1989, $136 billion; 1990, $100 billion; 1991, $64 billion; 1992, $28 billion; 1993, zero. Congressional Budget Office, *The Economic and Budget Outlook*, xv.

31. From the final product side of gross national product, $Y = C + I + G + X - M$, where Y is GNP, C is consumption, I is investment, G is government spending, X is exports, and M is imports. From the factor payments side of national accounts, $Y = C + S + T$, where S is saving and T is taxes. Subtracting the second equation from the first, and rearranging, $X - M = (S - I) + (T - G)$. The external balance thus equals the excess of private saving over private investment, plus the excess of tax revenue over government spending. The final bracketed term, the fiscal balance, thus has a direct accounting impact on the external balance.

of $150 billion would automatically eliminate an external deficit of the same size in the absence of other influences. A significant portion of the reduced fiscal deficit would tend to be offset by induced increases in domestic investment, as lower government borrowing reduces interest rates and encourages investment ("crowding in"). Lower interest rates could also raise private consumption, although if the fiscal deficit is reduced by higher taxes, private consumption would tend to decline as the result of lower disposable income.

Reduction of the fiscal deficit by $150 billion could thus reduce domestic demand (consumption plus investment plus government spending, $C + I + G$) by perhaps $75 billion to $100 billion. The marginal propensity to import (the fraction of each additional dollar of total demand that is spent on imports) in the United States is approximately one-fifth.[32] The reduction in domestic demand associated with elimination of the fiscal deficit would thus translate into a cutback in imports by some $15 billion to $20 billion, much less than the full $150 billion reduction in the fiscal deficit.

On the export side, lower interest rates in the United States could encourage other countries to lower their own interest rates, and could thus increase growth of foreign demand and stimulate US exports. In addition, lower domestic demand would tend to release some resources for increased exports. It is unlikely, however, that these indirect export effects would be as large as the direct import effects. Liberal allowance for export effects might boost the total impact of the fiscal adjustment on the trade balance to a range of $25 billion to $35 billion. By implication, with domestic demand down by $75 billion to $100 billion and the trade balance up by only $25 billion to $35 billion, respectively, domestic production would decline by $50 billion to $65 billion, or by 1 to 1½ percent of GNP.[33]

In short, fiscal adjustment is a necessary condition for US external adjustment, but by itself it is likely to be inadequate. As developed below, the US current account deficit needs to be cut from its prospective 1992 level of approximately $150 billion to some $50 billion. Reduction in the external

---

32. The average propensity to import, or the ratio of imports to GNP, is approximately 10 percent. The income elasticity of imports is approximately 2 (table A-3). The marginal propensity to import equals the income elasticity multiplied by the average propensity to import.

33. This discussion (but not necessarily the quantitative magnitudes) follows John Williamson, "Achieving a Sustainable Payments Position," Testimony before the Joint Economic Committee, US House of Representatives, 9 February 1989.

deficit by some $25 billion to $35 billion as the result of elimination of the fiscal deficit alone would achieve only one-fourth to one-third of this objective. Two other measures will be required: real depreciation of the exchange rate, and acceleration of foreign growth from the baseline outlook. This would essentially require merely the maintenance of high 1988 growth rates in key countries, as discussed below.[34]

Exchange rate change is fortunately a natural counterpart of fiscal adjustment. In the mainstream macroeconomic analysis for an open economy (for example, the Mundell–Fleming framework), fiscal contraction reduces the interest rate, which in turn reduces the inflow of capital from abroad. Lower capital inflows mean less foreign exchange bidding for dollars, and the exchange rate of the dollar declines.[35]

Just as fiscal adjustment without exchange rate adjustment is likely to be inadequate, so would be the reverse. Even if the exchange rate could be independently depreciated without fiscal adjustment, the results would be unfavorable. In this case, the resulting upward pressure on net exports without a reduction in domestic demand would cause an acceleration in inflation, risking a vicious circle of depreciation, inflation, and more depreciation in the attempt to maintain the real decline of the dollar. (This process has been witnessed in several Latin American countries that have attempted to adjust externally without adequate fiscal adjustment.) In contrast, a balanced package of fiscal adjustment and exchange rate reduction can help avoid the negative output impact of fiscal contraction alone. In the illustration above, US GNP declined by 1 to 1½ percent. By adding dollar devaluation to the policy

---

34. The need for exchange rate change to supplement fiscal adjustment (even when matched by fiscal expansion abroad) is forcefully argued in Paul Krugman, "Adjustment in the World Economy," Working Paper No. 2424 (Cambridge, Mass: National Bureau of Economic Research, 1988). The issue is essentially the classic transfer problem. The home country has a lower marginal propensity to spend on imports than on its own goods, as does the foreign country. Only a modest portion of fiscal contraction in the home country thus translates into lower imports, and a limited portion of fiscal expansion abroad translates into higher imports from the home country. The net reduction in demand in the home country and expansion abroad creates excess supply at home and short supply abroad. A change in the relative price, the exchange rate, is necessary to clear the markets.

35. Market sentiment might initially react to a firm announcement of US fiscal correction in just the opposite way, by bidding up the dollar on the grounds that the central flaw in economic policy was now being corrected. Eventually the influence of lower interest rates would be likely to dominate, however.

package, higher exports and lower real import volume can provide additional demand so that production need not fall.

In sum, a policy package containing US fiscal adjustment, real depreciation of the dollar, and some economic expansion abroad is likely to be required to achieve US external adjustment, and can permit adjustment without a slowdown in domestic growth or a recession.

MODEL SIMULATION OF POLICY CHANGES

The HHC and EAG models provide a basis not only for projecting the baseline outlook for US and foreign external accounts, but also for simulating the impact of policy changes.

Conceptual Issues—Three main variables drive both projection models: US GNP, the real exchange rate of the dollar, and foreign GNP. Neither model explicitly incorporates fiscal policy. Instead, it is implicitly assumed that the fiscal stance changes in a way that is consistent with the changed income and exchange rate variables applied in alternative policy simulations. In particular, there must be sufficient fiscal adjustment so that the postulated real depreciation of the dollar is not frustrated by rising inflation, which neutralizes nominal exchange rate changes.

In the HHC and EAG models, US GNP affects the US external accounts on the side of demand for imports. Faster growth spurs faster import expansion. Foreign GNP affects exports, as faster growth abroad increases demand for US exports. In terms of the impact of fiscal adjustment as outlined above, the models capture the reduction of the fiscal deficit (at an unchanged exchange rate) only insofar as the net reduction in domestic demand translates into reduction in GNP (production) and therefore imports. Similarly, they capture any non-exchange rate effects of fiscal adjustment on exports only through higher foreign growth (in response to lower world interest rates).

In practice, the "growth" variables in both models serve as proxies for a mixture of production ($C + I + G + X - M$, or GNP) on the one hand and domestic demand ($C + I + G$) on the other. A portion of imports is closely related to production: intermediate inputs into the manufacturing process. Another portion is more closely related to domestic demand: final goods (C) and capital goods (I). Empirical estimates over time estimated on the basis of GNP tend to capture both influences. Similarly, policy simulations that change "growth" to influence imports implicitly can change the mixture of output growth and domestic demand growth. Thus, if Japan increases government spending and Japanese consumption rises as the result of shorter work weeks and more leisure time, Japanese demand for US exports can rise even with an unchanged level of GNP in Japan. In this regard, the policy simulations that call for higher growth rates abroad should be interpreted to include higher growth of domestic demand instead of or as well as higher GNP. This interpretation is important, because it means that "growth" acceleration that might appear implausible in terms of actual output (because of capacity constraints) is feasible when understood in terms of domestic demand expansion.

The other central variable, the exchange rate, also raises questions of interpretation. The model simulations apply changes in the exchange rate independently (but, as noted, with the implicit assumption that fiscal policy changes in a compatible way). Some would ask whether it makes any sense in a floating rate world to consider the exchange rate as an independent variable. At a proximate level, the answer is affirmative. Especially since the Plaza Agreement of 1985 and the Louvre Accord of 1987, the industrial countries have in practice reverted to a system of central exchange rates with, apparently, relatively narrow bands. At successive meetings the Group of Seven (G-7) determines whether to reaffirm the existing exchange rates or change the targets. The system is essentially an unannounced target rate regime. Under these circumstances, the exchange rate has again become de facto a direct policy variable, in contrast to its benign neglect under more freely floating rates in the first half of the 1980s.

At a deeper level, however, the answer to whether the exchange rate can be treated as a policy variable for model simulation is that underlying fiscal and monetary policy are telescoped into the exchange rate variable. Despite the G-7 agreements, any alignment of exchange rates sharply at odds with interest rate differentials and inflationary expectations would be likely to collapse soon, as central bank intervention would be insufficient to sustain it. At this more fundamental level, then, the direct use of the real exchange rate variable in the policy simulations once again reaches back to the assumption that underlying fiscal (and monetary) policy is compatible with the real exchange rate specified.

Policy Impact Estimates—Table 5 shows the estimated impact of each "policy instrument"—exchange rate, foreign growth, and US growth—on the US trade and current account balances by 1992. The policy simulations

TABLE 5 Policy parameters for the United States (billions of current dollars except as noted)

						Change in 1992 trade						
	EAG model						HHC model					
Instrument	X	M	TB	TB/X%	CA	CA/X%	X	M	TB	TB/X%	CA	CA/X%
Exchange rate depreciation (1% real)												
Against all countries	7.2	-0.3	7.5	1.5	10.2	2.0	4.4	-0.8	5.2	0.9	7.8	1.4
Against strong countries only	3.7	-0.6	4.3	0.9	5.8	1.2	3.5	-0.5	4.0	0.7	5.6	1.0
Against strong countries + Canada	6.0	-0.5	6.5	1.3	8.9	1.8	3.7	-0.7	4.4	0.8	6.4	1.2
Increased foreign growth (1% for 1 year)												
In all countries	8.3	0.0	8.3	1.9	11.5	2.3	10.5	0.0	10.5	1.9	19.8	3.6
In strong countries	4.5	0.0	4.5	1.1	6.2	1.2	4.5	0.0	4.5	0.8	9.2	1.7
In strong countries + Canada	6.5	0.0	6.5	1.5	9.1	1.8	6.9	0.0	6.9	1.3	13.3	2.4
Decreased US growth (1% for 1 year)	0.0	-11.5	11.5	2.3	14.8	3.0	0.0	-11.0	11.0	2.0	15.0	2.7

X = change in exports; M = change in imports; TB = change in trade balance; CA = change in current account balance; TB/X% = change in trade balance as a percentage of 1992 exports; CA/X% = change in current account balance as a percentage of 1992 exports.

used to derive the parameters are a 10 percent real depreciation of the dollar phased in over the four quarters of 1989, and a change in baseline 1989–92 annual growth by 1 percentage point.

Real depreciation of the dollar by 1 percent against all foreign currencies increases the 1992 US trade balance by $7.5 billion in the EAG model and by $5.2 billion in the HHC model. The larger impact in the EAG model stems from its higher price elasticities for trade than in the HHC model. The corresponding effects for the current account are $10.2 billion and $7.8 billion. Thus, one-fourth to one-third of the total effect arises in the service sector—a point often missed by trade models. The HHC model in particular captures such effects as the change in valuation of direct foreign investment income resulting from a change in the exchange rate.

Because most developing countries are not in a position to allow their currencies to appreciate against the dollar, the simulations also examine exchange rate change against "strong" areas only, defined to include all of the industrial countries (including or excluding Canada), Taiwan, and Korea–Singapore–Hong Kong. A 1 percent real depreciation of the dollar against the strong countries including Canada increases the 1992 US current account balance by $8.9 billion in the EAG model and by $6.4 billion in the HHC model. (The special role of Canada is most evident in the EAG model.)

One-percentage-point higher growth for one year in the strong countries including Canada increases the 1992 US trade balance by $6.5 billion in the EAG model and by $6.9 billion in the HHC model. The corresponding current account effects are $9.1 billion and $13.3 billion, with the larger HHC estimate attributable primarily to higher earnings on US direct investment abroad when foreign growth accelerates.

The two models show practically identical effects of 1-percentage-point lower growth for one year in the United States: an increase in the 1992 trade balance by approximately $11 billion and in the current account balance by $15 billion.

These parameters provide an initial basis for gauging the dimension of the policy actions required. For example, if it is desired to reduce the 1992 US current account deficit from the base case estimate of $153 billion to only $50 billion, and if the average parameters for the two models are applied, acceleration of growth from the baseline by ¾ percentage point annually in 1989–92 in the strong countries including Canada would contribute $33 billion (¾ × 4 × $11 billion), and the remaining $70 billion could be obtained from real depreciation of the dollar against the same areas by 9.1

percent ($70 billion/$7.65 billion per percentage point). Acceptance of some reduction in US growth would permit either less growth acceleration abroad or a smaller dollar depreciation.

Unbalanced Distribution of Adjustment Abroad—As might be suspected from the emerging distortions in external balances of countries other than the United States, discussed above, a uniform application of exchange rate and growth policies places undue burdens on the weaker foreign countries, even when foreign adjustment is limited to the industrial countries (including Canada) and the East Asian NICs. Indeed, one of the most striking findings of the simulations using the EAG model is that if exchange rate or growth changes abroad are adopted uniformly across countries, the large surpluses of Germany and Japan essentially fail to decline; instead the full burden of the counterpart of lower US deficits is absorbed by declining external balances of the intermediate and weaker foreign countries.

Thus, with an across-the-board 10 percent appreciation of foreign currencies against the dollar by the strong countries,[36] Germany's 1992 trade balance remains unchanged from the baseline level at $107 billion, and that of Japan declines only marginally (from $128 billion to $122 billion); meanwhile the trade deficit of France rises from $13 billion to $20 billion, that of Italy from $7 billion to $13 billion, and that of the Other Industrial countries from $62 billion to $83 billion. This outcome is partly attributable to low price elasticities in Germany, but principally to what may be called the "balloon effect." Because Germany and Japan have sizable trade surpluses against the intermediate industrial countries in the baseline projections, even at unchanged trade volumes with these other countries a rise in the dollar price of German, Japanese, and other European goods due to the decline in the dollar causes the dollar value of the preexisting trade imbalances to balloon. The swelling of the dollar value of the German and Japanese surpluses against industrial countries other than the United States thus largely or fully offsets the decline in the surpluses of these two countries with the United States (and other dollar-area countries) resulting from the exchange rate change. In contrast, for the intermediate countries a rising deficit with Germany and Japan adds to the declining surplus with the United States to cause a twofold deterioration in their trade balances.

---

36. The uniform policy simulations exclude Canada from the adjustment.

The balloon effect also applies to changes in foreign growth rates, although in this case it is trade volumes rather than nominal values that swell. Thus, when all strong countries (excluding Canada) adopt an increase in their annual growth rates of 1 percentage point over four years, the 1992 trade balances of Germany and Japan remain virtually unchanged from their baseline levels, while the trade balance of France falls by $9 billion, that of Italy by $3 billion, and that of the Other Industrial countries by $16 billion. The German and Japanese surpluses with the intermediate countries in the base case mean that when relatively similar proportional increases in trade volumes occur as the result of uniform growth acceleration, the volume of the trade deficit expands. Once again, the balloon effect vis-à-vis the intermediate industrial countries neutralizes the trade balance reduction of Germany and Japan against the United States and the dollar-area countries, while compounding the deterioration of the intermediate countries against the dollar area.

Thus, exchange rate appreciations against the dollar and acceleration of growth rates (and/or increases in domestic demand) from baseline trends need to be differentiated by country if disparities between high-surplus Germany and Japan, on the one hand, and the intermediate countries, on the other, are to be avoided as a consequence of US external adjustment. Another important issue in the foreign impact of adjustment measures concerns the alternative of US growth reduction as the means of adjustment rather than exchange rate change or foreign growth acceleration. An obvious drawback of this option is the loss of GNP in the United States. An additional disadvantage, however, is the sideswiping of the developing countries. When US adjustment takes place through reduced growth, US imports decline not only from strong areas but also from the developing countries. If instead adjustment is achieved through exchange rate appreciation and higher growth in the strong areas, the developing countries obtain a windfall gain by improving their competitiveness as their exchange rates with the dollar remain unchanged. For example, the trade balance of the non-OPEC Latin American countries declines by $5 billion from its 1992 baseline when the United States grows more slowly by 1 percentage point over four years, whereas the region's trade balance rises by $7 billion from the baseline value when the strong countries (excluding Canada) appreciate by 10 percent, and by $6 billion when, alternatively, the strong countries accelerate growth above baseline by 1 percent over four years.

Because of the potential for US external adjustment to aggravate already emerging imbalances among other countries, it is important that an overall international adjustment strategy differentiate prospective policy action among various countries. In general, the most energetic measures in terms of exchange rate change and growth demand changes need to be focused on the countries with the largest surpluses. In the absence of such concentration, the burdens imposed on intermediate countries as a consequence of US external adjustment could incite resistance in these countries to that adjustment. In particular, these countries could oppose exchange rate appreciation and could resort to increased protection as the result of new balance of payments pressures.

5 An International Adjustment Program

The EAG projection model provides a basis for design and simulation of a package of policy measures to reduce the US external deficits in a manner that is compatible with an appropriate distribution of the counterpart adjustment by surplus countries, and thus with sustained global growth.

US CURRENT ACCOUNT TARGET

The first decision to be made in designing an international adjustment package is the appropriate level for the US external balance. The baseline deficit of some $150 billion by 1992 is almost certainly too high in view of the risks already outlined. Thus, Marris and Bergsten have both argued that a target of zero should be set for the current account balance.[37]

The analysis that follows indicates that even a less ambitious adjustment target would involve substantial real exchange rate appreciation and the maintenance of high rates of growth by Germany, Japan, and such countries as the Netherlands, Switzerland, and Belgium. The need to concentrate adjustment on these countries poses limits on the magnitude of adjustment

---

37. Stephen Marris, *Deficits and the Dollar* (1987 revision), 203; C. Fred Bergsten, *America in the World Economy*. Marris also notes that by the early 1990s the United States could be in current account surplus, but only if the dollar falls beyond its equilibrium level and the economy enters into recession (p. xxvii).

that are less apparent when the extent of adjustment is considered under uniform foreign measures.

At the same time, there are reasons to believe that a current account deficit in the range of $50 billion could be sustainable. Williamson argues that the target should be set at approximately 1 percent of US GNP by 1992, or $60 billion. He notes that, with US demographic growth higher than that in Europe and Japan, there is a case for capital inflow into the United States (although the more traditional position is that as a high-income country the United States should be a provider of capital to the rest of the world rather than a net user). With nominal GNP growing at 7 percent, holding the annual increment of net external debt to 1 percent of GNP would eventually stabilize the ratio of net external debt to GNP at 14 percent.[38]

A range of $50 billion for the 1992 current account deficit would also be consistent with relatively modest investment patterns by foreign investors. In 1987 and the first three quarters of 1988, gross US capital outflows amounted to an average of approximately $70 billion annually.[39] After allowance for inflation, these outflows by 1992 might be in the range of $85 billion annually. Foreign earnings on assets held in the United States are projected at $146 billion (table B-2). With a current account deficit of $50 billion and gross capital outflows of $85 billion, total financing requirements would amount to $135 billion annually. On this basis, passive reinvestment by foreigners of their annual earnings on assets held in the United States would be sufficient to cover US financing requirements.[40] Under the assumption that the overall portfolios of foreign investors would be growing at a rate at least as high as reinvestment of earnings, the share of US assets in their portfolios would hold steady or decline, avoiding the risk of satiation.

In sum, although a target closer to zero for the current account deficit might be more certain to dispel the risks of macroeconomic crisis, persistent interest rate pressure, and protectionism, an outcome in the range of

---

38. If dD is the change in foreign debt, dY the change in income, and Y income, then $dD = .01Y$, $dY = .07Y$, and $dD/dY = .14$. Thus, at the margin, new foreign debt is 14 percent of increased GNP. Under the adjustment scenario, 1992 net external debt is $843 billion (table B-2), or approximately 14 percent of GNP. With the marginal rate equal to the average, the ratio would stabilize at this level. John Williamson, "Achieving a Sustainable Payments Position."

39. *Commerce 1988:3 Current Account.*

40. Note that the specific HHC model projections call for a larger gross capital outflow in 1992, but still the rate of accumulation of foreign holdings in the United States (8.8 percent) remains close to the rate of passive reinvestment.

$50 billion by 1992 should be broadly manageable and might have some justification in view of demographic trends. The analysis of this study adopts this objective for the external sector.

PROGRAM DESIGN

The international adjustment program should take into account the fact that there are at least three adjustments that need to take place: reduction of the US external deficit, moderation of a large emerging deficit in the United Kingdom, and limitation of emerging deficits of intermediate European countries resulting largely from trade with Germany (and other high-surplus European countries: Belgium, the Netherlands, and Switzerland). The adoption of adjustment measures should be as broadly dispersed as possible, to obtain the largest possible scope for US adjustment, while recognizing the different tiers of strength of external accounts. In particular, the adjustment program is designed to ensure that no country is pushed into a current account deficit in excess of 10 percent of exports of goods and nonfactor services as a consequence of US external adjustment.[41]

Another principle of the adjustment program is that, if possible, adjustment through reduction in US growth should be avoided. The sacrifice of growth is a costly way to improve the external balance, and the baseline growth rate for the United States (2.8 percent in 1989 and 2.5 percent thereafter) is not so high as to call for reduction solely for anti-inflationary purposes.

Numerous simulations of the EAG model following these principles and seeking a $50 billion current account deficit target for the United States by 1992 yielded the Feasible Adjustment Package (FAP) set forth in table 6. The FAP involves a sharp appreciation of the German mark (23 percent) and the Japanese yen (28 percent) against the dollar in real terms from the base levels of 1987:4, to nominal rates of 1.33 DM/$ and 102 yen/$ by the end of 1989 (table 7) or, at the latest, equivalent real rates by the end of 1990 (as discussed below). The two countries would also accelerate their domestic economic growth (or at least the growth of domestic demand) by 1 percentage

---

41. In view of the decline of the US current account deficit to 6 percent of exports of goods and services in the FAP adjustment program proposed below, it would be anomalous to expect other countries to accept far higher external deficits as the counterpart of US adjustment, thereby potentially creating a new group of countries with deficit problems.

point annually from the baseline levels (from 2½ percent to 3½ percent for Germany and from 4 percent to 5 percent for Japan). In practice, the two countries would need only to sustain their high growth rates of 1988 over the next four years, rather than increase growth still further. The currencies of the two East Asian NIC areas, Taiwan and Korea–Singapore–Hong Kong, would also appreciate in real terms against the dollar, by 12 and 14 percent, respectively, although in view of their already high growth rates these countries would not accelerate domestic growth.

The Other Industrial countries would appreciate their currencies by an average of 13.5 percent in real terms, but in two subgroups: the currencies of the surplus European countries (the Netherlands, Belgium, and Switzerland) would appreciate by the same amount as Germany (23 percent), while those of the other industrial countries not individually analyzed (such as Sweden and Australia) would appreciate by only 5 percent. Similarly, growth would accelerate by 1 percent annually for the three stronger countries, and by only ½ percent annually for the weaker ones; the average increase in the growth rate for the Other Industrial countries would be 0.75 percent.

France and Italy would also appreciate their currencies by only 5 percent in real terms against the 1987:4 dollar, and accelerate growth by only ½ percent annually. As a result of divergent appreciation, there is a major realignment within the European Monetary System, with a rise of some 17 percent in the currencies of a strong deutsche mark bloc against the other member currencies. In the absence of this realignment, the German surplus tends to remain high, and the deficits of the intermediate European countries become large as the United States adjusts. The implications of EMS realignment are considered below.

Table 6 also shows exchange rate changes for the other areas identified in the EAG model. Because of their strong baseline trends, Brazil and the Rest of World group are able to match the currency appreciation and growth acceleration of the intermediate group; Canada and Mexico can make more modest adjustments in the same direction. All the other developing countries have underlying trends too weak to permit absorption of any of the counterpart to US adjustment, and therefore they keep their real exchange rates against the dollar and their baseline growth rates unchanged. The only country that should depreciate in real terms against the dollar is the United Kingdom, to address the severe negative trend in its external accounts.

The changes in growth rates in the FAP are spread evenly over 1989–92. The exchange rate changes are all implemented in 1989, with one-fourth of

TABLE 6   A Feasible Adjustment Package

	Measure	
Group	1989 real exchange rate appreciation against dollar[a] (%)	1989–92 annual growth increment above baseline (%)
Strong A		
Japan	28	1.0
Germany	23	1.0
Strong B		
Korea–Singapore–Hong Kong	14	0.0
Taiwan	12	0.0
Intermediate A		
Other Industrial	13.5	0.75
Intermediate B		
France	5	0.5
Italy	5	0.5
Brazil	5	0.5
Rest of World	5	0.5
Intermediate C		
Canada	3.5	0.25
Mexico	2.5	0.25
Weak A		
Argentina	0	0
OPEC	0	0
Other Africa	0	0
Other Latin America	0	0
Weak B		
United Kingdom	−3	0
United States	−10.7[b]	0

a. From 1987:4 base.
b. Real trade-weighted depreciation

the change introduced in each of the four quarters. Alternative simulations indicate that the exchange rate changes could instead be spread over two years (1989–90), to moderate the pace of their change, without major jeopardy to US external adjustment; the cost in terms of the 1992 current account deficit would be only $4 billion. However, further delay would cause a serious shortfall from the adjustment goals by 1992, in view of the two-year lags in the trade effects of exchange rate changes.[42]

Table 7 reports the real exchange rate changes on a trade-weighted basis. For the United States, the FAP depreciation amounts to 10.7 percent. For Germany, there is a trade-weighted real appreciation of approximately 15 percent; that for Japan is 21 percent. These changes are less traumatic than might be inferred from the larger appreciations of the mark and yen against the dollar in the package (23 and 28 percent, respectively). Trade-weighted real exchange rates actually depreciate by 4 to 5 percent for France and Italy, because of the importance of Germany and the stronger European countries in their trade. For Taiwan and Korea–Singapore–Hong Kong, trade-weighted appreciation is limited to a range of 3 to 5 percent, reflecting the importance of trade with Japan, whose currency appreciates by more than those of the East Asian NICs. The Other Industrial countries' currencies appreciate by 5 percent on a trade-weighted basis, but this figure results from averaging higher appreciation by the strong payments bloc and real depreciation by the intermediate countries.

Table 7 also reports the implied nominal exchange rates for 1989 corresponding to the targets for real exchange rate change. These estimates take account of differential inflation between the United States and each country. The nominal value of the German mark by the end of 1989 is set at 1.33 per dollar, and for the yen at 102 to the dollar. As indicated in the table, if the mark had stayed at its stronger level at the end of 1987, the required change in the nominal rate against the dollar would have been only

---

42. Spreading the exchange rate changes evenly over three years raises the 1992 US current account deficit by $38 billion from the unadjusted FAP program. Note that some models identify an adverse trend for US trade over time even when external accounts begin from approximate equilibrium, so that additional subsequent real depreciation might be required. There is no such adverse trend in the HHC model, and in the EAG projection model the unfavorable asymmetry between the trade-weighted, specific/uniform averaged income elasticities on the import and export sides (2.2 and 1.8, respectively) is more than offset by the differential in base case growth rates (2.6 percent annual average for the United States versus 3.7 percent abroad weighting by US exports).

T A B L E 7   **Exchange rate changes implied by the Feasible Adjustment Package**

Country/group	Change (real) against 1987.4 (%)	Nominal rate (currency units/dollar)			
		1987:4	12/31/87	8/15/88	11/17/88
United States					
Strong A					
Japan (yen/$)	28	135.8	123.5	132.2	122.3
Germany (DM/$)	23	1.706	1.582	1.879	1.727
Strong B					
Korea (won/$)	14	799.2	792.3	723.3	693.9
Taiwan (New Taiwan dollar/$)	12	29.5	28.5	24.0	28.0
Intermediate A					
Other Industrial	13.5				
France (FF/$)	5	5.755	5.34	6.38	5.9
Italy (lira/$)	5	1,248	1,169	1,394	1,287
Brazil (cruzado/$)	5	60.06	72.25	267.41	517.00
Rest of World	5				
Intermediate B					
Canada (Canadian dollar/$)	3.5	1.311	1.300	1.224	1.232
Mexico (peso/$)	2.5	1,784.6	2,209.7	2,281.0	2,300.0
Weak A					
Argentina (austral/$)	0	3.42	3.75	11.96	15.29
OPEC	0				
Other Africa	0				
Other Latin America	0				
Weak B					
United Kingdom (pound/$)	−3	0.570	0.534	0.583	0.547

a. Figures for the US represent depreciation of the dollar in trade-weighted terms.
b. Not calculated because of the high degree of uncertainty about domestic inflation rates.

FAP:1989	% nominal appreciation required by end-1989, from:				Trade-weighted real appreciation vs. dollar (%)[a]	
	1987:4	12/31/87	8/15/88	11/17/88	Bilateral weights	Multilateral weights
					-10.68	-10.63
102.3	32.8	20.7	29.2	19.6	22.36	20.32
1.327	28.6	19.2	41.6	30.1	14.93	15.39
680.6	17.4	16.4	6.3	2	4.61	5.04
24.6	19.9	15.9	-2.4	13.8	2.82	2.84
					2.82	5.33
5.32	8.2	0.4	19.9	10.9	-5.22	-4.48
1,171	6.6	-0.2	19.0	9.9	-4.62	-4.42
b	b	b	b	b	-1.08	-4.24
					-4.42	-4.80
1.268	3.4	2.5	-3.6	-2.8	0.01	-5.93
b	b	b	b	b	-1.01	-6.77
b	b	b	b	b	-7.92	-7.12
					-10.18	-9.62
					-8.39	-9.39
					-7.38	-9.36
0.578	-1.4	-7.6	1.0	-5.4	-13.74	-12.93

19 percent. Instead, because of the weakening of the mark against the dollar in 1988, the required change from the mid-November 1988 nominal rate amounts to 30 percent. Among the various countries, only Korea and Canada experienced exchange rate movements in 1988 that placed their rates at approximately the desired levels.

IMPACT OF ADJUSTMENT MEASURES ON EXTERNAL BALANCES

As Table 3 indicated, the Feasible Adjustment Package reduces the 1992 US current account deficit to $48 billion, meeting the $50 billion ceiling. This deficit amounts to 6 percent of US exports of goods and services. Because the baseline current account deficit in the EAG model is $168 billion in 1992, the amount of the correction is $120 billion, rather than the rounded adjustment of $100 billion from a broad range of $150 billion (the average of the HHC and EAG models) to the $50 billion target.

The reduction of the 1992 US current account deficit by $120 billion is the result of a trade-weighted real exchange rate depreciation by 10.7 percent and a weighted-average acceleration of foreign growth by 0.41 percentage point annually from baseline (or by 1.64 percentage-point-years). Application of the policy parameters of table 5 to these changes yields a current account change of 10.7 × $10.2 billion + 1.64 × $11.5 billion = $128 billion. The divergence is attributable to alteration in the policy parameters when the measures are not uniform but concentrated in the surplus countries. These calculations indicate that, of the total adjustment, 85 percent is from real exchange rate change and 15 percent from acceleration of foreign growth and/or domestic demand.[43]

---

43. Note that this decomposition leaves no room for an additive, independent effect of fiscal adjustment, although it was suggested above that the partial-equilibrium effect of a reduction in the US fiscal deficit by $150 billion could be a trade balance improvement of up to $35 billion (if domestic demand fell by $100 billion). The harmonization of the two approaches is as follows. The $15 billion increase in US exports hypothesized from the induced foreign interest rate reduction and resulting faster growth abroad may be seen as contained in the $19 billion increase in exports from foreign growth acceleration in the FAP simulation of the EAG model (suggesting that a major portion of this acceleration could occur automatically from lower interest rates abroad rather than require increased fiscal stimulus). The $20 billion reduction in imports hypothesized for lower US "domestic demand" from fiscal adjustment should probably be seen as half associated with lower imports of intermediate inputs because of declining US

A natural question is why an additional depreciation of the dollar by only some 10 percent, along with modest acceleration of foreign demand, would suffice to cut the external deficit to $50 billion when previous depreciation of the dollar had achieved far less adjustment. The dollar declined in real terms by almost 40 percent from its peak in 1985:1 through 1987:4 (against currencies of 18 major countries, using multilateral trade weights and deflating by foreign consumer prices and US export-weighted wholesale prices). The main answer is that if the dollar had remained at its real 1985:1 level, by 1992 the US current account deficit could have reached over $400 billion, on the basis of simulations with the HHC model. Most of the dollar's decline so far has served merely to prevent explosive growth of the deficit.

The difference between the trade and current account deficits for the United States in the adjustment scenario ($44 billion and $48 billion, respectively; table 3) is surprisingly small; in the base case, the current account deficit exceeds the trade deficit by $35 billion (EAG model). The explanation is that, for the United States, nonfactor service exports are higher relative to merchandise exports (29 percent) than are nonfactor service imports relative to merchandise imports (18 percent). Hence, when the merchandise trade gap narrows, there is a growing surplus on nonfactor services that largely offsets the deficit (of approximately $45 billion in the FAP case) on transfers and capital services.

Application of the FAP to the HHC model generates closely similar results for the trade deficit, which stands at approximately $40 billion in both models. However, the current account deficit resulting from the FAP in the HHC model is considerably smaller at only $18 billion (table B-2). None-theless, if account is taken of possible upward bias in the capital services projections in the HHC model because of the persistence of a large differential

---

production under fiscal contraction without exchange rate change, and half attributable to reduced domestic demand at constant output. Because addition of the 10 percent exchange rate decline reduces the real trade deficit by more than enough to prevent a decline in production, the first half of this partial-equilibrium fiscal effect on the import side disappears. The only remaining additive impact of the fiscal contraction per se, in the FAP scenario, is the $10 billion import cutback associated with reduced domestic final demand. In broader terms, however, the contribution of fiscal adjustment is far more important. By reducing domestic demand by $100 billion, it essentially makes room for the increase in the trade balance by approximately the same amount when the 10 percent real exchange rate depreciation is added. Otherwise the depreciation would cause overheating of the economy, rising inflation, and less external adjustment.

in the rates of return on new US direct investment abroad and foreign investment in the United States (as noted above), the two models generate similar current account estimates, both within the $50 billion target range.

Table 4 shows the distribution of adjustment in US trade by individual trading partner. The largest absolute improvements in US bilateral balances occur with Japan and the Other Industrial countries. The reduction of the US deficit with Japan from $60 billion in the base case in 1992 to only $30 billion augurs well for the potential of the adjustment package to relieve political pressure in the United States for protection against that country.[44] Large absolute contributions to improved US trade also come from Taiwan, Korea–Singapore–Hong Kong, Canada, and the Rest of World group. The most disappointing bilateral trend is in trade with Germany: the FAP actually widens the bilateral deficit from $12 billion to $17 billion, a reflection of the low price elasticities in US–German trade. However, protectionism against Germany has not been an issue, and bilateral balances per se have little importance except insofar as they fuel such political pressure.

The FAP has far more success than any of the uniform policy measures in reducing the outsized surpluses of Germany and Japan. Thus, by 1992 with the FAP Germany's current account surplus falls from a baseline $85 billion to only $16 billion, or from 16 percent of exports of goods and services to 3 percent. Japan's surplus is more resistant but nonetheless declines from the baseline $136 billion to $63 billion, from 34 percent of exports of goods and services to 16 percent.

For intermediate countries France and Italy, the FAP actually increases the 1992 current account balance from the baseline level, because of the trade-weighted depreciation of their currencies. The package thus addresses the emerging intra-European imbalance. In contrast, the East Asian NICs experience deterioration, although again their current account levels may be understated by dilution of their individually favorable trade elasticities through averaging with uniform elasticities. Even so their 1992 deficits remain at approximately the permitted limit of 10 percent of exports.

The developing countries generally experience increases in their current

---

44. Note that a $30 billion US bilateral trade deficit is close to the range identified by Bergsten and Cline as a structural equilibrium rate, in view of triangular trade and a more normal surplus position for the Japanese current account overall. C. Fred Bergsten and William R. Cline, *The United States–Japan Economic Problem*, POLICY ANALYSES IN INTERNATIONAL ECONOMICS 13 (Washington: Institute for International Economics, October 1985), 40.

account balances relative to the base case as a result of the FAP, because their fixed real exchange rates against the dollar and absence of growth acceleration above baseline mean that increased competitiveness in third-country markets more than offsets reductions in trade balances against the United States (as a result of US substitution for other country supply).

The FAP broadly achieves the intended concentration of the current account reductions in the high-surplus countries. Except for a small reduction in the position of Canada, only five countries or country groups experience lower surpluses or higher deficits compared with the baseline outcome: Japan (− $73 billion), Germany (− $69 billion), the Other Industrial countries (− $60 billion), Taiwan (− $7 billion), and Korea–Singapore–Hong Kong (− $20 billion). The principal shortfall from the extent of adjustment that might be desired is in the case of Japan, as discussed above (and some would argue that the persistence of a significant surplus in Japan is not inappropriate, on grounds that surplus savings from this high-savings country contribute to capital availability for global growth).[45]

ALTERNATIVE ADJUSTMENT PROGRAMS

If a more ambitious program to achieve zero US external deficit by 1992 is pursued, further dollar depreciation and/or foreign growth acceleration (or US growth deceleration) will be required. Because large currency appreciations

---

45. Note that the proportionate distribution of surplus reduction in the FAP resembles that recommended by a group of 33 economists in late 1987. In both cases, Germany absorbs approximately 30 percent of the total surplus reduction, and Korea and Taiwan together account for 12 to 14 percent. The principal differences are for Japan (32 percent in the FAP, versus 52 percent in the earlier study), and the Other Industrial countries (26 percent in the FAP versus none). The Japanese surplus is thus more resistant than had previously been anticipated, while there is a considerably larger role for such surplus European countries as the Netherlands, Switzerland, and Belgium than identified before. In addition, the absolute magnitude of the total surplus reduction is much larger (some $230 billion versus $125 billion), because of the addition of the objective of reducing a large emerging deficit in the United Kingdom (and to a lesser extent Italy and France) to the underlying goal of reducing the US external deficit, on the one hand, and because of the larger baseline surpluses in Japan and Germany than in the 1987 base used in the earlier study, on the other hand. Institute for International Economics, *Resolving the Global Economic Crisis: After Wall Street*, SPECIAL REPORT 6 (Washington: Institute for International Economics, December 1987), 17.

are already called for in the more moderate FAP for Germany, Japan, Belgium, the Netherlands, and Switzerland, it is implausible that the additional necessary adjustment to reach a zero US external balance could similarly be concentrated in these countries. Instead, the Zero Balance Package (ZBP) increases the amount of currency appreciation by all countries appreciating in the FAP (except Mexico) by a flat 4 percentage points, and in addition increases the annual growth acceleration by ¼ percentage point beyond the FAP increment over four years in all the industrial countries. The resulting calculations show a heavy burden of adjustment on Canada in particular, but relatively modest further adjustment beyond the FAP case for other intermediate countries such as France and Italy. Nonetheless, several countries might consider the ZBP to impose excessive adjustment on them (for example, the yen would experience real exchange rate appreciation against the dollar of 32 percent).

Another alternative approach would seek to moderate the realignment of exchange rates within the European Monetary System, and moderate the large appreciations of the German and Japanese currencies with respect to the dollar, while still accomplishing the US external adjustment called for in the FAP. Political reaction in Europe and Tokyo could well be expected to push in this direction. For this purpose, a Second-Best Adjustment Package (SBAP) limits the appreciation of the yen to 20 percent in real terms against the 1987:4 dollar, and that of the mark to 18 percent. In contrast, the SBAP raises the appreciation of the currencies of the intermediate European countries from 5 percent in the FAP to 8 percent, and adds another percentage point appreciation beyond the FAP for Canada, Mexico, Rest of World, and Brazil. Other measures remain unchanged from the FAP.

The result of the SBAP is a 1992 US current account deficit that only slightly exceeds the target (at $52 billion), but much larger current account surpluses in Germany ($32 billion) and Japan ($87 billion) than under the FAP, and considerably larger deficits in the intermediate countries ($9 billion for France, $18 billion for Italy, and $77 billion for the Other Industrial countries); there is also serious trade deterioration for Canada compared with the FAP outcome. As expected, this lesser concentration of the policy adjustment results in poorer achievement of the objective of concentrating the counterpart of US adjustment in the high-surplus countries.

IMPLICATIONS FOR INTERNATIONAL ADJUSTMENT POLICY

These simulation results have several major policy implications. For the United States:

● An appropriate policy target is to reduce the US current account deficit to $50 billion by 1992. Complete elimination of the deficit could require adjustment beyond the degree acceptable to other, especially high-surplus, countries. A $50 billion deficit would represent less than 1 percent of GNP; would permit a stable or falling foreign debt-to-GNP ratio; would probably require only the passive reinvestment of foreign earnings on investments in the United States rather than additional inflows beyond this amount; and, if used for capital investment, could be an appropriate use of international savings in view of relatively high US demographic growth.

● Fiscal adjustment that meets the goals of the Gramm–Rudman–Hollings legislation, which calls for reduction of the federal deficit by $40 billion annually over four years, is the sine qua non for US external adjustment. In its absence, exchange rate depreciation will tend to raise inflation, undermining the extent of real exchange rate decline.

● Both models used in this study (HHC and EAG) indicate that further real depreciation of the dollar by approximately 10 percent beyond its 1987:4 level will be required to achieve the $50 billion current account target, as well as moderate acceleration of growth abroad (or maintenance of recent high growth rates, in Germany and Japan).

● Once the United States has cut back its external deficit to this range, the current account deficit should not greatly exceed the trade deficit, as a surplus on nonfactor services offsets the sizable deficit on transfers and investment income.

● Political pressure for protection against Japan—a considerable threat with a baseline bilateral deficit of $60 billion by 1992—should be ameliorated by the reduction of this deficit by half under the FAP, as should protectionism more generally with reduction of the overall trade deficit to $44 billion.

For foreign countries:

● An appropriate set of measures can achieve reduction of the US current account deficit to $50 billion by 1992 without imposing severe strain on the external accounts of other individual countries (and with any resulting deficits limited, in most cases, to no more than 10 percent of exports of goods and services).

- For this purpose, however, it is necessary to concentrate foreign adjustment measures heavily in the high-surplus countries: Germany, Japan, Belgium, the Netherlands, and Switzerland, and to a lesser extent, Taiwan and Korea. Otherwise, there will be an undue burden on countries in intermediate payments positions.

- Even with such concentration (including 28 percent appreciation of the yen), Japan's current account surplus in 1992 remains at a relatively high $60 billion, and appropriate financial recycling of this surplus (ideally including more lending to developing countries) remains of particular importance for this country.

- The need for larger appreciation by Germany and Japan than by intermediate countries means that a realignment of up to 17 percent is called for between a strong deutsche mark bloc within the European Monetary System (EMS) including Germany, Belgium, and the Netherlands, on the one hand, and other members such as France and Italy, on the other. Otherwise external sector pressures on the intermediate European countries will be burdensome as the United States seeks to adjust. A second-best policy limiting the intra-EMS realignment to 10 percent could still permit the United States to meet its external adjustment target, but would imply larger imbalances within Europe and the need for greater financial flows from surplus to deficit countries in the EMS.

- The United Kingdom faces special problems of severe external sector deterioration and cannot contribute to US adjustment. The United Kingdom can instead take advantage of exchange rate realignments and depreciate modestly against the dollar, and thus sharply against the mark and the yen, to reduce its external deficit trend dramatically (table 3).

- The developing countries can safely weather, and indeed benefit from, US external adjustment by keeping real exchange rates unchanged against the dollar and becoming more competitive in third markets. The trade gains under international adjustment are prospectively the largest for those developing countries with export markets concentrated in Europe (especially Germany) and Japan.

For international policy coordination among the G-7 industrial countries:

• Both models show that foreign growth matters importantly to US adjustment, contrary to those who argue that foreign expansion has so little effect on US external accounts that policy coordination cannot contribute much to US adjustment.[46]

• G-7 exchange rate stabilization efforts beginning with the Louvre Accord in 1987 were premature because the dollar remained overvalued in real terms. The failure of US and Japanese authorities to intervene energetically against the brisk rise in the dollar following the Toronto summit in mid-1988[47] was highly questionable, in view of the fact that the dollar had already risen after the end of 1987 and the need instead for a trade-weighted decline of the dollar by approximately 10 percent from its 1987:4 level (or 5 percent from its December 31, 1987, level).

• G-7 exchange rate policy has tended to set relatively narrow ranges around current exchange rates (after the Louvre Accord). The need for a much more sharply differentiated set of exchange rate changes means that this policy should allow for wider changes and facilitate substantially differing changes of individual currencies against the dollar, rather than implicitly expect all industrial country currencies to move in tandem against the dollar.

Two final issues of policy strategy warrant special discussion. The first concerns second-best strategy in the United States; the second, the role of the European Monetary System in international adjustments. The central policy package includes both fiscal adjustment and additional exchange rate depreciation for the United States (as well as increased growth abroad). Skeptics about the political feasibility of US fiscal adjustment must ask whether, in its absence, the second-best policy package should nonetheless include dollar depreciation along the lines proposed here. The Federal Reserve by early 1989 was clearly opposed to further dollar depreciation in the absence of fiscal correction, and indeed by moving toward higher interest rates out of fear of an overheating economy, the Fed showed itself prepared to allow the dollar to rise further rather than seek its decline.

---

46. For example, Martin Feldstein, "The End of Policy Coordination," *Wall Street Journal,* 9 November 1988.
47. *Wall Street Journal,* 28 June 1988, 3.

If the painful choice posed by this "second-best" question cannot be avoided, the conventional answer would be that the Federal Reserve is right to fight inflation at all costs and allow the US dollar and American external deficits to rise. However, relegation of the external deficit to a minimal policy priority in the past, far behind price stability and growth, has already placed the US economy in potential jeopardy for the reasons set forth at the outset. At some point US authorities may find it necessary to revise their policy weights on growth, inflation, and external balance, or else risk far greater recessionary and inflationary shocks in the future because of failure to act promptly on the external imbalance.

With respect to the European Monetary System, some observers note an increasing determination among countries with weaker payments positions, such as France, to maintain an essentially fixed exchange rate with the German mark. In this perspective, these countries have enjoyed macroeconomic gains from adherence to a German-led "zone of stability" that they do not want to jeopardize. Some even contend that the intra-EMS exchange rate realignment suggested here would "destroy" that system. The move toward more complete integration in Europe by 1992 contributes to this insistence on unchanged parities, as it implies not only possible strengthening of monetary integration but also an increasing tendency to view intragroup payments imbalances as of no greater concern than, for example, imbalances between individual states within the United States.

The analysis of this study, and particularly the simulation applying uniform appreciation of exchange rates by other industrial countries against the dollar, indicates that, if members of the EMS are firmly determined to avoid exchange rate realignment among each others' currencies, the surplus countries (especially Germany) will have to be prepared to provide large amounts of financing on an ongoing basis to the members with deficits. Although a case might be made that such transfers are desirable for European economic growth, the central point from a global standpoint is that pursuit of these intra-EMS objectives should not impose a roadblock to international adjustment, and to US external adjustment in particular.

6   Real Adjustment in the United States and Abroad

The analysis presented in this study indicates that, with decisive but reasonable policy action in the United States and other major countries, it should be possible to achieve reduction in the US external deficit to sustainable levels over the medium term. However, it is important to go beyond the financial analysis to examine the implications of deficit reduction for real magnitudes of trade, production, and consumption. It is these real volumes that affect employment and production.

REAL VERSUS NOMINAL ADJUSTMENT

Real trade and economic changes associated with US external adjustment are likely to differ from nominal dollar changes. Because some 25 percent cumulative inflation is likely from the base year 1987 through 1992, from this standpoint real changes should be smaller than nominal changes. However, because of adverse changes in the terms of trade—that is, in the ratio of export prices to import prices—as the dollar declines, the real changes can considerably exceed the nominal changes. In particular, the nominal dollar value of imports is unlikely to change much even as the volume of imports is reduced by higher dollar prices, because the same rise in the dollar price that stimulates the reduced purchases also raises the unit price and tends to leave the total dollar outlay on imports unchanged. Although there is some offsetting gain from a rise in dollar prices of exports, this induced price rise tends to be smaller than that on imports. In broad terms, most of the work of external adjustment must be accomplished on the side of increased export volume. In real terms, this increase must be added to the reduction in import volume (which is largely invisible in financial terms because of the rise in the dollar price of imports) to gauge the total shift in real resources that must be mobilized to accomplish external adjustment.

A simple model of the relationship of real to nominal external adjustment shows that, given the empirical trade elasticities and tendencies to pass through exchange rate changes into prices, the real trade balance must rise by almost twice as much as the nominal trade balance when adjustment is accomplished by exchange rate depreciation.[48] An objective of reducing the

---

48. Specifically:

$Z = [-Hda - eb]/\{[-Hda - eb] + [H(1 - a)(1 - dar) - b(1 + ebr)]\}$, where Z is the ratio of real to nominal adjustment, H is the base period ratio of exports to imports, a is the pass-through ratio from dollar depreciation to dollar import prices, b is the pass-through ratio for export prices, d is the price elasticity of foreign demand for US exports, e is the price

nominal external deficit by $100 billion through exchange rate adjustment thus requires a combination of real import volume reduction and real export volume expansion amounting to nearly $200 billion at constant prices, or some 4½ percent of US GNP.

REAL EFFECTS OF TRADE IMBALANCES IN THE 1980S

External adjustment thus can serve as a major source of demand for the US economy over the medium term. The opposite was true through much of the 1980s. From 1980 to 1986, the real trade balance on goods and services declined from a surplus of $57 billion to a deficit of $138 billion (at constant 1982 prices). The decline of the real external balance thus reduced external demand during this period by an amount equal to 6 percent of 1980 GNP.[49] Over the same period, the real balance on nonoil, nonagricultural trade declined by an amount equivalent to 23 percent of 1980 manufacturing value added. Despite offsets by domestic consumption and rising defense expenditure, manufacturing production and especially employment suffered during the 1980s as the result of the collapse of net demand from the external sector. Indeed, these adverse real trends mounted the pressure for protection that eventually forced the Reagan administration to shift its approach from commending the strong dollar to seeking its reversal, as formalized in the 1985 Plaza Agreement.

The reverse side of the coin was a large stimulus from US demand to the economies of major trading partners. From 1980 to 1986, the rise in Japan's real trade balance accounted for 26.3 percent of Japan's total increase in real GNP, and for Germany trade contributed 52 percent of growth. The rise in the real bilateral trade balance with the United States in this period accounted

---

elasticity of US demand for imports, and r is the proportionate change in the exchange rate. Note that as a rises from zero to unity, the exchange rate change impact rises from zero effect on the dollar price of imports to complete effect. As b rises from zero to unity, a given dollar depreciation causes a full corresponding rise in dollar export prices (none of the benefit of lower foreign currency price of the dollar is passed through to foreign purchasers) to zero rise (complete pass-through of this benefit). Applying the average values in the HHC and EAG models for the trade elasticities and price pass-through ratios, Z has an average value of 1.9.

49. Calculated from Council of Economic Advisers, *Economic Report of the President,* February 1988, 250, 261, 271.

for approximately one-half of the total trade contribution to growth for both countries. More specifically, the rise in the real trade balance with the United States from 1980 to 1986 amounted to 2.4 percent of 1980 GNP for Germany and 3.4 percent for Japan. The corresponding figure for Canada was 10.5 percent, and the impact was even higher in Taiwan and Korea. For the world as a whole, the rise in real trade balances against the United States from 1980 to 1986 amounted to 2.1 percent of 1980 non-US global GNP. A central challenge of US external adjustment over the medium term is whether the reversal of US demand for the rest of the world's goods, from a positive to a negative stimulus, can be absorbed by other countries without a serious reduction in their growth rates.[50]

PROSPECTIVE REAL ADJUSTMENT IN THE UNITED STATES

The simulations of FAP adjustment using the HHC and EAG models confirm that real US external adjustment through 1992 to achieve the $50 billion nominal current account deficit target amounts to approximately $200 billion at 1987 prices. This adjustment of 4½ percent of 1987 real GNP over four years means that domestic demand will have to be restrained relative to growth of production, with the growth in demand lagging that of GNP by approximately 1 percentage point annually.[51] With production growing at a rate of 2½ percent annually, domestic demand for consumption, investment, and government spending should rise by only 1½ percent each year.

Because investment should grow at least as fast as GNP (to maintain capital stock relative to GNP) and perhaps faster (to the extent that external adjustment requires a reallocation of the economy toward tradeable goods, which tend to be more capital intensive than nontradeables such as retail

---

50. An important ameliorating factor in the challenge foreign countries face because of the large shift from positive to negative demand stimulus from trade with the United States is the accompanying reversal of US fiscal–monetary mismatch. In the mid-1980s, high US interest rates spilled over into foreign economies and acted as a drag, partially offsetting the stimulus from rising real trade surpluses with the United States. Future US fiscal correction could moderate world interest rates and help offset the adverse demand impact on other countries' economies from US external adjustment.

51. This useful formulation appears in C. Fred Bergsten, *America in the World Economy*, 7–8, 84.

sales and other services), consumption and government spending should probably grow by only about 1 percent annually.[52] As the population is growing at this rate as well, per capita consumption and government spending per person should remain frozen in real terms over the next four years to accommodate external adjustment. This freeze, after rapid growth in the 1980s (by 2.3 percent annually from 1980 to 1987, for both real per capita consumption and real per capita government spending),[53] is in many ways the principal "burden" of US external adjustment. It represents a period of correction after what amounted to a spree of private and public consumption during the 1980s, financed by foreigners.

Although the real external adjustment implies domestic belt-tightening, it also signifies dynamism in precisely the sectors of the economy that were under the greatest pressure from faltering external demand in the earlier years of the decade. Most of the increase in the trade balance will have to occur in the manufacturing sector. If the entire rise took place in manufacturing, it would amount to approximately 16 percent of 1987 manufacturing GNP. With 4 percent annual manufacturing growth over 1989–92 needed to meet external demand and another 1½ percent annually for rising domestic demand, the sector should grow at over 5 percent annually, or more than twice its 2.5 percent average rate from 1980 to 1986. This pace is sufficiently brisk to raise the question of whether manufacturing capacity will be sufficient, but with trend capacity growth at 2½ percent and some initial excess capacity in 1988, capacity shortages should not be a major problem (although they could be a constraint in some specific sectors such as rubber, chemicals, aerospace, and paper).[54]

By 1987 and 1988 the process of positive demand stimulus from a declining real trade deficit had already begun in the United States. In 1987 the real

---

52. With gross investment equal to 16 percent of GNP, if investment grows at 3 percent annually and domestic demand (consumption plus investment plus government spending) can only grow at 1½ percent, then growth of consumption and government spending must be limited to 1.2 percent $[.015 - (.16 \times .03)]/.84 = .012$.

53. Council of Economic Advisers, *Economic Report of the President,* January 1989, 310–311.

54. Robert Z. Lawrence, "The International Dimension," in Robert E. Litan, Robert Z. Lawrence, and Charles L. Schultze, eds., *American Living Standards* (Washington: Brookings Institution, 1988), 23–65.

nonagricultural, nonoil trade deficit declined from $124 billion to $116 billion, and in 1988 the deficit fell further to $79 billion (at 1982 prices).[55] This trend illustrated the divergence between real and nominal adjustment, as the real deficit declined in 1987 even as the nominal deficit continued to rise. It also was an early indication of the demand stimulus that could be anticipated for manufacturing if US external adjustment continued. In the two years, the decline in the real nonoil, nonagricultural trade deficit amounted to approximately 5 percent of 1987 manufacturing GNP. Nonetheless, it was an ominous sign that the decline in the real trade deficit stopped by the second quarter of 1988 (when the nonoil, nonagricultural trade balance at 1982 prices stood at an annual rate of $74.4 billion), and began a small reversal thereafter (to $76.3 billion by the fourth quarter).

THE GLOBAL IMPACT OF US ADJUSTMENT IN REAL TERMS

Table 8 provides estimates of the impact of real external adjustment on the economies of other countries that may be expected in the base case and under successful US external adjustment as called for in the FAP. As shown, the real impact is negligible for Germany and Japan in the base case, but large in the case of the FAP. Successful US external adjustment by 1992 along the lines developed here would mean a reduction in the real trade balance of Germany amounting to 7.3 percent of 1987 GNP, and in that of Japan by 4.1 percent. The negative real demand effect would also be high in the Other Industrial country group (-7.3 percent), and even higher in Taiwan and Korea–Singapore–Hong Kong.[56] The impact of real adjustment abroad is especially high if compared to manufacturing production, reaching -23.9 percent in Germany and -13.5 percent in Japan.

The real impact of the adjustment program on the high-surplus countries is pronounced. In real quantities Germany's imports rise by 34 percent in

---

55. US Department of Commerce, *Gross National Product: Fourth Quarter 1988 (Preliminary)*, BEA-89-05 (Washington: US Department of Commerce, 28 February 1989).

56. Although in the East Asian NICs the relative impact tends to be exaggerated because the base should ideally include imported intermediate inputs (which are particularly important for comparisons with manufacturing alone) as well as GNP. Note also that the US figure of 3.7 percent of GNP real adjustment in the table is lower than the 4½ percent discussed above because it refers to merchandise trade alone and excludes nonfactor services.

T A B L E 8   **Changes in real nonoil trade balances, 1987–92, relative to 1987 production**
(billions of 1987 dollars except as noted)

| Country/group | 1987 Production | | Real trade balance change | | Trade balance change as % of 1987 | | | |
| | | | | | GNP | | Mfg. | |
	GNP	Mfg.	Baseline	FAP	Baseline	FAP	Baseline	FAP
United States	4,526.7	997.4	60.8	166.6	1.3	3.7	6.1	16.7
United Kingdom	669.6	174.1	-48.1	0.7	-7.2	0.0	-27.6	0.0
France	878.3	193.2	-7.0	5.4	-0.8	0.6	-3.6	2.8
Germany	1,125.6	360.2	2.4	-82.4	0.2	-7.3	0.7	-22.9
Italy	751.5	165.3	-9.8	4.0	-1.3	0.5	-5.9	2.4
Canada	402.0	68.3	-3.0	-5.4	-0.8	-1.3	-4.4	-7.9
Japan	2,290.8	687.2	-4.9	-93.0	-0.2	-4.1	-0.7	-13.5
Argentina	72.8	22.6	1.7	3.1	2.3	4.3	a	a
Brazil	250.5	70.1	9.8	11.3	3.9	4.5	a	a
Mexico	149.2	38.8	-4.6	-4.2	-3.1	-2.8	a	a
Taiwan	99.4	38.8	-15.0	-20.8	-15.1	-20.9	-38.7	-53.6
Other Industrial[b]	1,149.3	n.a.	-26.4	-83.6	-2.3	-7.3	n.a.	n.a.
Korea–Singapore–Hong Kong	179.7	49.6	-25.0	-47.1	-13.9	-26.2	-50.4	-95.0
Other Latin America[b]	133.3	n.a.	3.7	12.5	2.8	9.4	n.a.	n.a.
Other Africa[b]	211.5	n.a.	0.6	12.2	0.3	5.8	n.a.	n.a.
Rest of World[b]	2,685.3	n.a.	37.3	61.1	1.4	2.3	n.a.	n.a.

a. Not applicable; exports not primarily manufactured goods.
b. 1986 production data.
n.a. not available.

Sources: William R. Cline, *United States External Adjustment and the World Economy*; World Bank, *World Development Report 1988*; IMF, *International Financial Statistics*, October 1988; OECD, *National Accounts: 1974–1986, Vol. II Detailed Tables*; Taiwan District, Republic of China, *Financial Statistics*, October 1988; Republic of China, *Taiwan Statistical Data Book 1987*.

the base case from 1987 to 1992, but by 57 percent under the FAP, while Germany's export expansion falls from 24 percent in the baseline to 11 percent. Real imports rise by 54 percent over the period in the base case for Japan, but increase by 85 percent under the FAP, while Japan's real export expansion declines from 24 percent in the base case to − 1 percent under the FAP.

For the United Kingdom, the international adjustment program works in the opposite direction, and prevents what otherwise would be a baseline reduction of the real trade balance equal to 7.2 percent of GNP. Real correction through the adjustment program is thus proportionately larger for the United Kingdom than for the United States.

It is evident from table 8 that relatively large negative real demand effects must be anticipated in other countries (especially the high-surplus countries) as the United States carries out external adjustment. It will be necessary for these countries to replace their export-led growth of the early 1980s with growth led by domestic demand. Since 1986 there have been initially encouraging signs that this transition is under way. Thus, whereas Japan's GNP growth exceeded that of its real domestic demand by 0.9 percentage point in 1985, by 1986–88 domestic demand growth exceeded that of GNP by an average of 1.4 percent annually. In Germany, the corresponding shift was from − 1.1 percentage point (domestic demand growth less GNP growth) in 1985 to 1.3 percent annually in 1986–87, although the differential slowed to 0.3 percent in 1988. The danger is that these trends toward international adjustment will stall as the pipeline effects of dollar devaluation become exhausted, as implied by the minimal real adjustment for these surplus countries over the 1987–92 period in the base case (table 8).

7 Policy Implications

The analysis of this study indicates that the United States is far from being on an acceptable course of correction of its external deficits, despite the reduction of the trade deficit by some $30 billion in 1988 and the prospects of a substantial further reduction in 1989. The trade and current account deficits are likely to remain above $100 billion in 1989 and then, absent policy change, to begin to widen again, with the current account reaching a deficit of approximately $150 billion again by 1992. This outlook threatens a macroeconomic crisis from an eventual collapse of confidence by foreign investors, with a hard landing for both the dollar and the economy. It condemns the economy to high interest rates to attract foreign financing, and thus prospectively low investment and growth. And it runs the risk of a renewed outbreak of protectionism. Moreover, the outlook in the absence of policy action is for further aggravation of existing distortions in international payments, with current account surpluses of nearly $140 billion in Japan and $85 billion in Germany by 1992, while deficits emerge in such intermediate countries as France, Italy, and especially the United Kingdom.

UNITED STATES

Correction of the US deficit must begin at home, with a new phase of restrained private and government consumption following the consumption binge of the 1980s. A coordinated package of fiscal policy, for spending restraint, and exchange rate policy, to provide the proper price signals for expenditure switching, is required.

Fiscal Policy—The single most important measure for the United States to adopt is the actual fulfillment of the Gramm-Rudman-Hollings targets, which call for reduction of the fiscal deficit by $40 billion annually to zero by 1993.

Exchange Rate Policy—In addition to fiscal measures, to reduce the current account deficit to a sustainable $50 billion by 1992 it will be necessary to reduce the real trade-weighted value of the dollar by approximately 10 percent from its level as of the fourth quarter of 1987, which was approximately the same as its level at the end of 1988 and in early 1989. US and foreign officials missed an important opportunity when they supported a rebound of the dollar from its low of December 31, 1987, and presided over a counterproductive rise of the dollar through the third quarter of 1988. From its end-1987 level, the dollar would have needed to decline by only about an additional 5 percent.

Macropolicy Mix—Reduction of the fiscal deficit will exert a contractionary influence on the economy, while dollar depreciation and the increase in the real trade balance will exert an offsetting expansionary influence. On the basis of 16 leading macroeconomic models of the United States, Bryant, Helliwell, and Hooper (BHH) calculate that reduction of the US fiscal deficit by 1 percentage point of GNP causes a 2 percent decline in the real value of the dollar, as the consequence of lower interest rates and reduced capital inflows bidding for dollars. They also find that a 1 percent rise in the stock of money causes a real decline in the dollar by 1 percent. They estimate that a fiscal contraction amounting to 1 percent of GNP cuts real GNP by 1 percent by the third year, and that a 1 percent rise in the stock of money increases GNP by ¼ percentage point.[57]

On this basis, a macroeconomic mix broadly consistent with the FAP strategy for reducing the US external deficit to $50 billion by 1992 would be as follows.[58] Implementation of Gramm–Rudman–Hollings amounts to a fiscal cut of approximately 3 percent of GNP. This measure should thus reduce the real value of the dollar by 6 of the nearly 11 percentage points called for in the FAP, while at the same time exerting a potential contractionary effect of 3 percent on GNP. To obtain the remaining real dollar depreciation of approximately 5 percentage points, and to provide an expansionary effect to help offset fiscal contraction, it would be appropriate to increase the money stock over 4 years by 5 percentage points more than would otherwise be the case, for example by raising the target for annual money growth from a range of 5 to 6 percent to a range of 6¼ to 7¼ percent.

The combined impact would be contractionay, based on the BHH parameters $[(-3\% \times 1) + (5\% \times 0.25) = -1.75\%]$, and GNP would decline from its baseline by approximately 0.4 percent annually over four years. However, as discussed above, the real effect of the FAP on US production is in the range of $200 billion (at 1987 prices), or more than the fiscal cutback rather than less, and the BHH relationships may be biased toward contraction. In practice, the fiscal–monetary mix just outlined could appropriately be altered in the direction of greater monetary expansion if the signs of inflationary trends in early 1989 proved to be transitory and fiscal contraction appeared

57. Ralph C. Bryant, John F. Helliwell, and Peter Hooper, "Domestic and Cross-Border Consequences of US Macroeconomic Policies," (Washington: Brookings Institution, Conference on Macroeconomic Policies in an Interdependent World, December 12–13, 1988).

58. Note, however, that as illustrated by the sharp decline in the dollar from 1985:1 through 1987:4 without massive fiscal and monetary adjustment, the relationship of the dollar to macropolicies is less than ironclad. If the policy mix indicated here failed to bring the dollar down sufficiently (for example, because of a short-term boost to confidence because the United States was finally correcting its fiscal imbalance), it seems likely that a policy of "jawboning" would be adequate to set the dollar in the proper range. If necessary, US authorities could reinstate a withholding tax on foreign earnings in the US capital markets to back up its verbal guidelines.

to be reducing growth, whereas monetary expansion could be cut back if the inflationary danger turned out to be serious and persistent. The central thrust of the macroeconomic mix over the next four years, however, should be to return policy toward a more normal configuration, after several years of an unusual (and, for the external sector, damaging) combination of loose fiscal policy and tight monetary policy.

GERMANY, JAPAN, AND THE SURPLUS EUROPEAN COUNTRIES

The two largest surplus countries, Germany and Japan, need to follow essentially two policies to fulfill their role in international adjustment: first, they should maintain over the next four years relatively high rates of growth of GNP and, especially, domestic demand similar to those they achieved in 1988; second, they should facilitate rather than oppose real appreciation of their currencies against the dollar by about 23 and 28 percent, respectively (and on a trade-weighted basis by 15 and 20 percent, respectively), as analyzed in this study. The other high-surplus European countries—Belgium, the Netherlands, and Switzerland—should follow policies parallel to those of Germany. These growth and domestic demand policies would essentially boost the rates of expansion by 1 percentage point annually above the baseline that could otherwise be expected.

To some extent these objectives could be facilitated by the package of US measures outlined above, which would tend to reduce US interest rates. There would be some induced reduction in interest rates in other countries as a result, contributing to maintenance of brisk domestic growth.

It is quite possible, however, that maintenance of buoyant growth of production and domestic demand will require greater fiscal expansion than currently planned in these countries. On balance there has been no movement toward fiscal stimulus in Japan, where the cyclically adjusted fiscal stance actually tightened by 0.7 percent of GNP in 1986, loosened by 0.5 percent in 1987, and tightened again by 0.2 percent in 1988.[59] The boost to Japanese demand and growth in 1987 from real wealth effects of the rising yen and the stock market boom cannot be expected to persist. The monetary expansion in Germany and Japan, which in part reflected coordinated support of the dollar, could be the object of increasing concern by monetary authorities

---

59. *OECD Economic Outlook*, June 1988, 24.

because of its possible inflationary consequences. In view of the major contractionary effects to be expected in the high-surplus countries as the counterpart of the US external correction, policymakers in these countries may find it necessary to turn to fiscal stimulus not only to play their part in international adjustment but also to avoid a domestic downturn.

EAST ASIAN NICS

Taiwan and Korea can fulfill their role in international adjustment by sustaining high domestic growth rates (in the range of 8 percent annually) and accepting the substantial real appreciations of their exchange rates suggested in the adjustment program reviewed above. As indicated in table 7, by late 1988 Korea had already largely accomplished the appropriate real appreciation of its exchange rate, although Taiwan had not.

The likelihood is that the surpluses of Taiwan and Korea will remain somewhat higher than projected in the EAG model, for reasons discussed above (higher export elasticities and lower import elasticities than used in the model's central projections). If the surpluses do persist, aggressive liberalization of imports would be the appropriate response, followed by additional exchange rate appreciation if necessary.

Although Hong Kong and Singapore are included in the same country grouping with Korea in the EAG model, it is unlikely that corresponding real appreciation of exchange rates would be appropriate for these two countries. Neither has incurred large current account surpluses in recent years of proportions comparable to those of Taiwan and Korea.

INTERMEDIATE INDUSTRIAL COUNTRIES

Perhaps the principal policy breakthrough needed in countries such as France and Italy is reassessment of the strongly held view that the existing fixed exchange rates in the European Monetary System are inviolable. As discussed above, a major realignment of rates within the EMS between the weaker members and the stronger bloc (Germany, Belgium, the Netherlands) appears necessary if severe pressure on the weaker members is to be avoided as the United States adjusts externally. If a lesser realignment (limited to 10 percent, for example) is all that is feasible politically, it will have to be accompanied by larger financing from the surplus members. It is imperative that Europe not turn toward protection as the consequence of insistence on maintenance of existing EMS exchange rates despite their prospective incompatibility with payments equilibrium for the weaker European countries, especially in an environment of US external correction.

DEBTOR COUNTRIES

The Latin American and other debtor countries stand to gain from the program of international adjustment outlined here. Their export opportunities should rise if they hold real exchange rates constant against the dollar and thus gain in competitiveness in the European and Japanese markets. Importantly, the debtor nations stand to gain from the lower international interest rates that should result from US fiscal correction. Real interest rates could drop from recent levels of some 5 percent to historically more normal levels of approximately 3 percent. A decline of 2 percentage points in international interest rates would save approximately $10 billion annually on the variable-interest debt of the developing countries. They could be expected to respend more than one-third of these savings on purchases of exports from the United States.

In addition, measures to reverse partially the large swing toward negative resource transfers from the debtor countries following the debt crisis could contribute to their economic growth as well as to international adjustment.[60] Simulations with the EAG model indicate that the provision of an additional $20 billion annually in effective finance (or cash flow relief from appropriate voluntary debt relief) at 1987 constant dollars would permit an improvement in the US current account by approximately $10 billion (nominal) by 1992.

---

60. Although the debt crisis probably played only a moderate role in the deterioration of the US external accounts in the 1980s, ranging from a trade balance deterioration of $12 billion (most probable) to a maximum of $25 billion on the basis of comparison against alternative benchmarks for what otherwise could have been expected of US trade with debtor countries.

Annex A
The HHC and EAG Models

Table A-1 presents the most important equations of the HHC model, and the full set of equations for the EAG model. Table A-2 presents the corresponding definitions of variables. Both models apply lag structures that give symmetrical, inverted-U weights stretching over seven or eight quarters (with the weight peaking at the middle of the lag period).

Table A-3 presents summary trade-weighted elasticities in the EAG model, based on the disaggregated elasticities by trading partner. It may be noted that an unfavorable income elasticity asymmetry is present for the United States in the EAG model (import elasticity = 2.44, export = 1.7) but absent in the HHC model (import = 1.098 + 0.992 = 2.09; export = 2.198). In projections the EAG asymmetry is diluted by averaging with the uniform income elasticity (1.97). The presence of the capital stock variable in the HHC model removes the income elasticity asymmetry by capturing rising foreign supply relative to that of the United States in past years.

The first four equations of table A-1 are the basic price and trade quantity equations of the HHC model. The fifth is included because of its importance in the services sector, as it illustrates the impact of both foreign growth acceleration and exchange rate change on capital services earnings.

63

TABLE A-1   **Model equations**

HHC Model

H1. $\ln P_x = -0.150 + 1.046 \ln P_{xw} + 0.214 \ln (P_{18}/E_{18})$

H2. $\ln XQ = -7.256 + 0.785 \ln D_x + 2.198 \ln Y_w + 1.358 \ln k_{t-1}$
     $- 0.822 \ln (P_x/[P_{18}/E_{18}])$

H3. $\ln P_m = 4.291 + 0.862 \ln P_{18} - 0.903 \ln E_{18} + 0.166 \ln P_c$

H4. $\ln MQ = -2.291 - 0.286 \ln u_{t-1} + 0.810 \ln D_m$
     $+ 1.098 \ln Y + 0.992 \ln Y_{t-1} - 0.837 k_{t-1}$
     $- 1.147 \ln (T P_m/P_d)$

H5. $\ln X_{Kdm} = 6.278 \ln [Y_f/Y_f^*] + 0.0565 \ln [K_{dm, t-1} P_{18}/E_{18}] + H$

EAG Model

E1. $\ln q_{ijt} = \alpha_{ij} + \beta_{ij}(\ln Y_{jt}) + \delta_{ij}(\sum_k w_k \ln [P_{i, t-k}/P_{j, t-k}])$
     $+ \sigma_{ij} (\sum_k w_k \ln [P_{Ni, t-k}^i/P_{i, t-k}])$.

E2. $P_{Ni}^i = (\sum_h \phi_h^i P_h)/(1 - \phi_i^i)$, where $h \neq i$

E3. $V_{ijt} = P_{it} q_{ijt}$

E4. $V_{ojt} = [V_{oj, t-1}] [P_t^o/P_{t-1}^o] \{1 + [(Y_{jt}/Y_{j, t-1}) - 1]\beta_o\}$

E5. $V_{o1t} = V_{o1t}^* \{1 + [(Y_{1t}/Y_{1t}^*) - 1] \beta_o^U\}$

E6. $V_{i, OP, t} = \phi_i^o \sum_j V_{OP, j, t}$

See table A-2 for explanations of the variables.

TABLE A-2   **Explanation of variables used in the equations of the two models**

Variable	Explanation
Equation H1	
P_x	Price of nonagricultural exports
P_{xw}	Average of US sectoral wholesale price indices weighted by export shares
P_{18}	Index of consumer prices in 18 foreign countries (bilateral US nonagricultural export weights)
E_{18}	Exchange rate index for the same 18 countries (multilateral trade weights); note that the ratio P_{18}/E_{18} includes a four-quarter lag)
Equation H2	
XQ	Volume of nonagricultural exports (1982 prices)
D_x	Variable for dock strikes
Y_w	Index of world GNP (bilateral US nonagricultural export weights, 1982 = 100)
k	Ratio of index of US capital stock to index of foreign industrial countries' capital stocks
	Note that the final term, using P_x, includes an eight-quarter lag.
Equation H3	
P_m	Price of nonoil imports
P_{18}	As in equations H1 and H2 but with bilateral nonoil import weights
E_{18}	As in equations H1 and H2 but with import weights (and with a seven-quarter lag)
P_c	Index of commodity prices
Equation H4	
MQ	Volume of nonoil imports (1982 prices)
u	Ratio of capacity utilization in 10 industrial countries to capacity utilization in the United States
D_m	Variable for dock strikes
Y	US GNP
T	Influence of the tariff on import prices
P_d	US GNP deflator
	Note that the final term, using P_m, includes a seven-quarter lag.
Equation H5	
X_{Kdm}	Investment income from US direct investment abroad in manufacturing
Y_f	Foreign GNP (investment-weighted)
Y_f^*	Corresponding potential output
K_{dm}	Real direct investment abroad in manufacturing
H	Set of constants for the various quarters and a dummy variable for 1981

TABLE A-2   **Explanation of variables used in the equations of the two models** (*Continued*)

Equation E1

q_{ij} Volume of exports from country i to country j

Y_j Real income in country j

β_{ij} Income elasticity of demand for country i exports to country j

w_k Weight given to the value for the period $(t - k)$ within the composite variable

P_i Dollar export price of country i

P_j Price of the competing domestic good in the importing market, country j

δ_{ij} Price elasticity of demand for country i exports to country j
Note that the ratio P_i/P_j includes a seven-quarter lag.

P_{Ni}^j Weighted price of all competing (i.e., non-i) suppliers of country j

σ_{ij} Cross-price elasticity of demand for country i exports to country j, for price relative to that of other exporters to the same market
Note that the ratio P_{Ni}^j/P_i includes a seven-quarter lag.

Equation E2

P_h Dollar export price of the hth other supplier to the jth market

ϕ_h^j Share of country h in imports of country j

Equation E3

V_{ij} Dollar value, at current prices, of exports from country i to country j

Equation E4

V_{oj} Dollar value of exports of oil from either OPEC, United Kingdom, or Mexico to country j

P^o Exogenous price of oil

β_o Income elasticity of demand for oil (set at 0.5 for all except the United States)

Equation E5

V_{o1} Dollar value of exports of oil from either OPEC, United Kingdom, or Mexico to the United States (asterisks indicate baseline projection values for oil imports and income)

β_o^U Income elasticity of demand for oil in the United States (set at unity)

Equation E6

$V_{i,OP}$ Forecasted dollar value of exports from country i to OPEC

ϕ_i^o Share of country i in total exports to OPEC (during 1985–87)

TABLE A-3 Country-specific trade elasticities and trade-weighted averages

Country/group	Import elasticities		Export elasticities			Difference of income elasticities[a]	Sum of price elasticities[b]
	Income	Price	Income	Price	Substitution		
United States	2.44	-1.36	1.70	-1.09	0.65	-0.74	3.10
United Kingdom	2.35	-1.04	1.79	-0.67	0.40	-0.56	2.11
France	2.68	-0.57	1.79	-0.42	0.32	-0.89	1.31
Germany	2.26	-0.48	2.04	-0.51	0.30	-0.22	1.29
Italy	2.48	-0.49	2.61	-1.10	0.49	0.13	2.08
Canada	2.01	-2.35	1.57	-1.01	0.37	-0.44	3.73
Japan	1.21	-0.69	2.24	-0.90	0.38	1.03	1.97
Argentina	2.42	-0.32	1.54	-0.36	0.33	-0.88	1.01
Brazil	0.42	-0.56	2.29	-0.61	0.53	1.87	1.70
Mexico	1.69	-0.51	2.92	-1.33	0.33	1.23	2.17
Taiwan	1.31	-0.42	2.70	-1.88	0.61	1.39	2.91
Other Industrial	2.26	-0.50	1.91	-0.60	0.54	-0.35	1.64
Korea–Singapore– Hong Kong	1.33	-0.32	2.66	-1.20	1.46	1.33	2.98
Other Latin America	1.62	-0.45	1.32	-0.50	0.31	-0.30	1.26
Other Africa	0.73	-0.32	1.00	-1.12	0.43	0.27	1.87
Rest of World	1.13	-0.47	1.80	-0.31	0.74	0.67	1.52
Trade-weighted average	1.97	-0.77	1.97	-0.77	0.55	0	2.09

a. Export minus import.
b. Absolute value; includes cross-price elasticity.

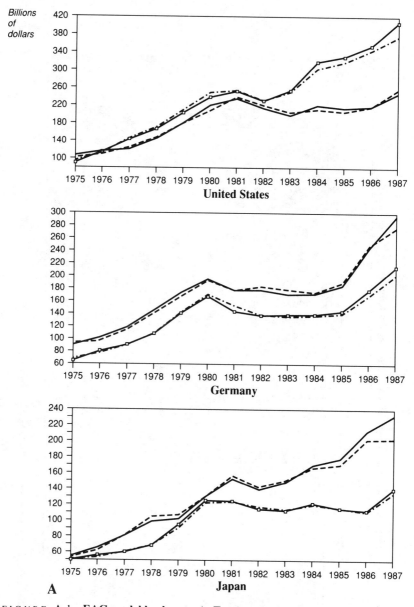

Billions of dollars

United States

Germany

Japan

A

FIGURE A-1   **EAG model backcasts. A: Total trade; B: bilateral trade. ——— ,
Exports, actual; ━ ━ ━ , exports, predicted; ∘━━∘ , imports, actual;
·—··— , imports, predicted.**

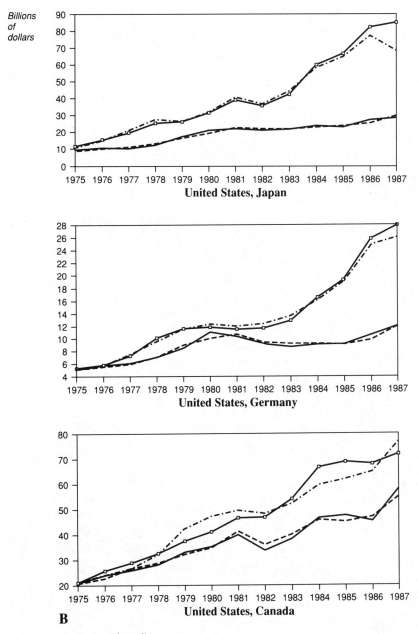

Billions of dollars

United States, Japan

United States, Germany

United States, Canada

B

FIGURE A-1   **(continued)**

Annex B
Statistical Tables

TABLE B-1 **US balance of payments, actual and projected (HHC, base case), 1980–92** (billions of dollars)

	1980	1981	1982	1983	1984	1985
Merchandise exports	224.27	237.08	211.20	201.82	219.90	215.93
Agricultural	42.16	44.03	37.23	37.14	38.40	29.57
Nonagricultural	182.11	193.05	173.97	164.68	181.50	186.36
Volume	201.81	198.23	173.97	167.60	184.29	195.60
Deflator	90.27	97.42	99.98	98.25	98.50	95.28
Merchandise imports	249.78	265.09	247.67	268.90	332.42	338.08
Oil	79.41	77.79	61.27	54.99	57.31	50.39
Nonoil	170.37	187.29	186.40	213.91	275.11	287.69
Volume	173.06	184.96	186.38	219.20	285.24	307.44
Deflator	98.49	101.28	100.01	97.62	96.47	93.57
Trade balance	−25.51	−28.00	−36.47	−67.08	−112.52	−122.15
NONA	11.75	5.76	−12.43	−49.23	−93.60	−101.33
Services exports	118.22	139.42	138.37	132.72	140.87	144.64
Factor	72.51	86.41	83.55	77.25	85.91	88.84
DI income	37.15	32.55	21.38	20.50	21.22	33.20
Other private	32.80	50.18	58.05	51.92	59.46	50.13
Gov't	2.56	3.68	4.12	4.83	5.23	5.50
Nonfactor	45.71	53.00	54.83	55.47	54.96	55.80
Services imports	83.27	97.09	101.65	102.41	123.32	122.59
Factor	42.12	52.33	54.88	52.38	67.42	62.90
DI income	8.64	6.90	3.16	5.60	9.23	6.08
Other private	20.89	28.55	33.44	28.95	38.42	35.52
Gov't	12.59	16.88	18.28	17.83	19.77	21.31
Nonfactor	41.15	44.76	46.76	50.03	55.90	59.69
Services balance	34.94	42.32	36.72	30.31	17.55	22.05
Factor services	30.39	34.08	28.67	24.87	18.49	25.93
Unilateral transfers	−7.59	−7.46	−8.96	−9.48	−12.10	−15.01
Current account	1.84	6.86	−8.70	−46.25	−107.08	−115.11
As % of GNP	0.07	0.23	−0.26	−1.36	−2.84	−2.87
Net external assets	95.10	129.99	125.73	78.48	−7.46	−122.97
Claims on foreigners						
DI	215.38	228.35	207.75	207.20	211.48	229.75
Other private	301.19	392.73	508.63	553.45	564.81	588.78
Gov't	79.37	87.60	97.39	102.14	108.70	119.75
Foreign claims on US						
DI	83.05	108.71	124.68	137.06	164.58	184.62
Other private	270.12	313.32	391.39	462.18	511.83	633.92
Other on gov't	147.67	156.66	171.98	185.07	216.03	242.72

DI = direct investment; NONA, nonagricultural, nonoil.

1986	1987	1988	1989	1990	1991	1992
223.97	249.57	338.98	404.24	445.84	496.06	553.64
27.36	29.52	29.11	31.21	33.46	35.88	38.46
196.61	220.05	309.87	373.03	412.38	460.18	515.17
212.99	237.42	315.74	353.05	371.80	395.22	421.47
92.33	92.66	97.99	105.63	110.89	116.41	122.20
368.52	409.85	466.86	505.14	553.21	611.71	670.07
34.39	42.88	38.96	46.21	56.18	63.91	72.36
334.13	366.97	427.90	458.93	497.03	547.80	597.72
346.35	365.40	379.24	359.19	375.53	392.19	411.20
96.44	100.40	112.99	127.77	132.33	139.66	145.33
− 144.55	− 160.28	− 127.88	− 100.90	− 107.37	− 115.65	− 116.43
− 137.52	− 146.91	− 118.03	− 85.90	− 84.65	− 87.62	− 82.54
151.09	175.26	178.90	189.92	202.19	216.02	232.40
90.11	103.76	100.93	103.99	109.69	117.07	126.63
38.42	52.31	46.45	54.76	63.20	72.45	82.77
45.27	46.12	50.51	45.46	42.70	40.71	39.85
6.42	5.33	3.96	3.77	3.78	3.91	4.01
60.98	71.50	77.97	85.93	92.51	98.95	105.77
130.06	155.50	176.22	190.30	205.02	221.10	238.78
66.97	83.38	104.37	114.15	123.44	133.91	145.50
5.38	10.51	18.55	21.16	23.46	25.93	28.72
38.98	48.83	61.58	68.80	74.71	81.38	88.89
22.61	24.05	24.25	24.19	25.27	26.60	27.89
63.09	72.11	71.84	76.15	81.58	87.18	93.28
21.03	19.76	2.68	− 0.38	− 2.83	− 5.07	− 6.38
23.14	20.37	− 3.45	− 10.16	− 13.76	− 16.84	− 18.87
− 15.31	− 13.44	− 13.00	− 13.59	− 14.21	− 14.86	− 15.54
− 138.83	− 153.97	− 138.20	− 114.87	− 124.41	− 135.59	− 138.36
− 3.28	− 3.43	− 2.83	− 2.19	− 2.22	− 2.26	− 2.15
− 274.63	− 453.46	− 591.65	− 706.52	− 830.93	− 966.52	− 1,104.88
259.89	261.02	303.93	345.24	384.42	423.36	463.11
670.03	711.87	582.73	538.08	509.82	490.93	488.57
126.90	116.59	116.59	116.59	116.95	116.95	116.59
209.33	251.31	272.91	297.99	326.91	360.32	398.59
831.36	966.37	1,019.50	1,105.40	1,202.19	1,311.27	1,434.19
290.76	325.27	302.49	303.04	312.66	325.82	340.37

TABLE B-2   **US balance of payments, projected (HHC, Feasible Adjustment Package), 1988–92** (billions of dollars)

	1988	1989	1990	1991	1992
Merchandise exports	339.15	410.08	477.01	553.24	624.17
Agricultural	29.11	31.21	33.46	35.88	38.46
Nonagricultural	310.04	378.87	443.55	517.36	585.70
Volume	315.91	357.19	394.36	437.80	472.16
Deflator	97.99	106.03	112.42	118.13	124.01
Merchandise imports	466.86	510.25	555.81	606.45	660.88
Oil	38.96	46.21	56.18	63.91	72.36
Nonoil	427.90	464.04	499.63	542.54	588.52
Volume	379.24	352.48	346.75	349.59	362.99
Deflator	112.99	131.70	144.09	155.18	162.11
Trade balance	− 127.71	− 100.17	− 78.80	− 53.22	− 36.71
NONA	− 117.86	− 85.17	− 56.08	− 25.18	− 2.82
Services exports	179.01	198.54	215.96	241.11	271.85
Factor	101.01	111.91	120.15	136.48	159.34
DI income	46.53	62.40	72.27	85.97	101.86
Other private	50.52	45.74	44.11	46.60	53.47
Gov't	3.96	3.77	3.78	3.91	4.01
Nonfactor	78.00	86.63	95.80	104.63	112.51
Services imports	176.22	190.37	204.41	219.77	237.12
Factor	104.37	114.44	123.78	134.05	145.55
DI income	18.55	21.16	23.46	25.93	28.72
Other private	61.58	68.80	74.71	81.38	88.89
Gov't	24.25	24.48	25.61	26.74	27.94
Nonfactor	71.84	75.93	80.63	85.72	91.57
Services balance	2.79	8.16	11.54	21.34	34.74
Factor services	− 3.36	− 2.53	− 3.63	2.43	13.79
Unilateral transfers	− 13.00	− 13.59	− 14.21	− 14.86	− 15.54
Current account	− 137.92	− 105.59	− 81.47	− 46.74	− 17.52
As % of GNP	− 2.83	− 2.02	− 1.45	− 0.78	− 0.27
Net external assets	− 591.37	− 696.97	− 778.44	− 825.18	− 842.70
Claims on foreigners					
DI	303.98	354.46	403.23	451.84	500.79

TABLE B-2   *continued*

	1988	*1989*	*1990*	*1991*	*1992*
Other private	582.96	544.82	546.00	604.77	713.44
Gov't	116.59	116.59	116.59	116.59	116.59
Foreign claims on US					
DI	272.91	297.99	326.91	360.32	398.58
Other private	1,019.50	1,105.40	1,202.19	1,311.27	1,434.19
Other gov't	302.49	309.46	315.16	326.80	340.75

DI = direct investment; NONA, nonagricultural, nonoil.

TABLE B-3   **Trade matrix, 1987** (billions of dollars)

Exporter	Importer							
	US	UK	FR	GE	IT	CA	JA	AR
US	0.00	14.11	7.94	11.75	5.53	57.36	28.25	1.09
UK	16.26	0.00	11.31	13.61	6.22	2.57	2.39	0.02
FR	10.48	12.61	0.0	23.81	17.34	1.47	2.21	0.29
GE	27.88	25.75	35.48	0.00	25.71	2.65	5.90	0.94
IT	11.10	8.46	18.45	21.17	0.00	1.35	1.88	0.38
CA	70.78	2.26	0.81	1.23	0.63	0.00	5.25	0.08
JA	85.02	8.48	4.06	12.96	2.12	5.66	0.00	0.45
AR	0.96	0.08	0.14	0.41	0.25	0.07	0.23	0.00
BR	7.67	0.95	1.14	2.02	1.32	0.64	1.87	0.67
ME	13.96	0.24	0.28	0.37	0.04	0.75	0.18	0.15
TA	24.62	1.50	1.11	2.15	0.67	1.53	6.48	0.01
OP	21.95	2.40	5.65	5.44	9.27	1.06	25.19	0.05
UP	1.94	0.00	1.52	1.83	0.59	0.61	0.07	0.00
MP	4.70	0.12	0.33	0.00	0.09	0.14	1.32	0.00
OI	31.37	47.84	47.94	83.72	26.30	3.99	14.58	0.80
KS	38.89	4.54	2.04	5.54	1.43	2.73	13.50	0.11
OL	11.67	1.24	0.91	2.14	0.88	0.69	1.47	0.80
AN	4.61	2.43	5.02	3.74	3.65	0.35	3.30	0.05
RO	21.37	9.75	9.56	20.68	11.95	1.69	21.08	0.24
Totals								
Exports	250.39	131.24	148.53	294.17	117.99	97.03	231.33	6.40
Imports	405.21	142.76	153.69	212.56	113.98	85.31	135.15	6.12
Trade balance	−154.82	−11.52	−5.15	81.60	4.02	11.73	96.18	0.28

US, United States; UK, United Kingdom; FR, France; GE, Germany; IT, Italy; CA, Canada; JA, Japan; AR, Argentina; BR, Brazil; ME, Mexico; TA, Taiwan; OP, OPEC; UP, United Kingdom-oil; MP; Mexico-oil; OI, Other Industrial; KS, Korea–Singapore–Hong Kong; OL, Other Latin America; AN, Other Africa; RO, Rest of World.

				Importer				
BR	ME	TA	OP	OI	KS	OL	AN	RO
4.04	14.58	7.41	10.56	33.60	16.14	11.67	3.34	23.02
0.57	0.33	0.48	7.84	35.14	3.35	1.30	3.66	13.07
0.88	0.35	0.46	5.78	41.71	2.16	2.94	7.72	18.33
1.49	0.83	1.49	7.99	114.85	3.87	2.25	4.97	32.13
0.42	0.18	0.41	12.27	27.96	1.68	0.99	2.74	8.56
0.48	0.40	0.58	1.16	3.54	1.37	0.89	0.50	7.09
0.89	1.00	11.45	11.51	23.37	28.32	5.19	3.40	27.47
0.52	0.06	0.26	0.30	1.07	0.08	0.71	0.31	0.95
0.00	0.14	0.09	1.52	2.82	0.56	1.67	0.46	3.10
0.22	0.00	0.17	0.06	1.34	0.24	0.84	0.06	0.65
0.03	0.07	0.00	2.08	2.35	5.75	0.96	0.84	3.08
3.61	0.01	2.47	2.07	14.03	7.84	3.45	1.92	19.41
0.00	0.00	0.00	0.00	6.57	0.00	0.00	0.00	0.00
0.00	0.00	0.00	0.00	0.57	0.00	0.00	0.00	0.00
1.24	1.24	2.66	5.57	121.76	8.17	4.29	6.78	50.69
0.12	0.19	1.65	4.15	9.31	8.02	1.84	1.79	28.51
0.91	0.10	0.38	0.51	10.68	0.39	2.69	0.16	1.86
0.22	0.04	0.83	0.57	6.48	0.55	0.42	3.10	13.32
0.83	0.09	3.99	10.67	34.26	25.68	0.84	4.08	85.85
26.61	26.78	53.22	125.82	458.93	124.37	37.49	48.71	262.61
16.48	19.61	34.78	84.60	491.40	114.16	42.95	45.82	337.08
10.13	7.18	18.45	41.22	−32.46	10.21	−5.47	2.88	−74.47

TABLE B-4   **Baseline trade projections, 1992** (billions of dollars)

Exporter	US	UK	FR	GE	IT	CA	JA	AR
				Importer				
US	0.00	31.89	16.05	21.27	9.86	110.27	58.85	2.32
UK	24.04	0.00	17.63	21.96	10.14	3.68	3.59	0.04
FR	17.75	23.76	0.00	37.26	29.29	2.03	4.10	0.55
GE	43.30	43.76	56.76	0.00	40.91	3.59	9.54	1.57
IT	16.71	15.29	30.76	34.61	0.00	1.83	3.34	0.64
CA	121.06	4.16	1.60	2.16	1.18	0.00	9.20	0.19
JA	119.36	14.58	6.22	19.40	3.32	8.28	0.00	0.83
AR	1.96	0.15	0.25	0.82	0.56	0.14	0.50	0.00
BR	14.91	1.78	2.20	3.20	2.65	1.05	3.37	1.21
ME	21.59	0.71	0.45	0.64	0.08	0.89	0.40	0.15
TA	29.41	2.38	1.21	3.09	0.91	1.98	12.53	0.02
OP	30.83	2.58	6.04	5.80	9.92	1.14	28.08	0.06
UP	3.94	0.00	1.63	1.95	0.63	0.66	0.08	0.00
MP	8.30	0.13	0.35	0.00	0.09	0.15	1.47	0.00
OI	43.10	81.31	81.60	138.59	44.80	5.27	22.35	1.45
KS	67.71	10.06	3.94	10.17	2.81	4.50	27.82	0.19
OL	20.13	2.24	1.77	4.01	1.75	1.15	2.96	1.17
AN	9.04	4.66	8.39	6.25	6.67	0.51	5.81	0.12
RO	31.50	17.94	20.86	37.34	24.91	3.58	41.46	0.68
Totals								
Exports	500.92	195.00	244.99	455.68	183.64	169.67	363.18	13.69
Imports	624.63	257.37	257.70	348.53	190.46	150.71	235.44	11.17
Trade								
balance	−123.73	−62.37	−12.71	107.16	−6.82	18.96	127.73	2.52

For an explanation of country abbreviations see table B-3.

			Importer					
BR	ME	TA	OP	OI	KS	OL	AN	RO
6.79	29.34	19.27	14.27	67.40	39.75	21.95	9.39	42.25
0.61	0.40	0.80	9.51	54.31	6.48	1.87	6.34	17.72
1.32	0.57	0.99	8.28	66.00	4.07	5.02	14.73	29.27
2.19	1.33	2.72	10.63	176.41	7.31	2.93	8.82	43.92
0.67	0.33	0.88	10.89	45.50	3.80	1.83	4.74	11.82
1.03	0.59	1.84	1.42	6.37	3.57	1.58	1.01	12.72
1.56	1.35	21.87	15.96	40.30	54.22	7.51	5.09	43.30
0.99	0.13	0.84	0.55	2.32	0.18	1.31	0.59	2.41
0.00	0.36	0.26	2.54	6.29	1.47	3.55	1.40	5.59
0.58	0.00	0.47	0.08	2.11	0.64	1.69	0.13	1.85
0.05	0.09	0.00	2.54	3.35	11.97	1.47	1.64	4.90
4.03	0.02	2.98	0.00	14.92	9.45	3.85	2.14	21.67
0.00	0.00	0.00	0.00	6.99	0.00	0.00	0.00	0.00
0.00	0.00	0.00	0.00	0.60	0.00	0.00	0.00	0.00
2.04	1.71	6.30	13.18	203.36	16.17	7.08	13.02	70.85
0.22	0.27	3.85	5.23	17.42	20.28	3.50	3.46	54.83
1.60	0.21	1.09	0.72	21.43	2.62	4.92	0.63	4.82
0.56	0.06	1.90	0.74	12.22	1.67	0.67	5.78	19.56
2.40	0.55	10.05	13.98	66.85	63.72	1.55	7.13	157.22
51.80	43.54	77.51	143.50	752.17	236.26	73.21	84.61	501.73
26.63	37.28	76.12	110.49	814.15	247.38	72.28	86.04	544.72
25.17	6.26	1.40	33.00	−61.98	−11.11	0.93	−1.42	−42.99

TABLE B-5   **Trade projections under the Feasible Adjustment Package, 1992**
(billions of dollars)

Exporter	Importer							
	US	UK	FR	GE	IT	CA	JA	AR
US	0.00	33.32	18.28	27.08	11.05	124.27	76.34	2.66
UK	25.52	0.00	20.47	28.05	11.67	3.92	5.74	0.06
FR	18.81	24.42	0.00	47.85	33.00	2.12	5.16	0.58
GE	44.19	39.34	62.56	0.00	45.08	3.59	12.03	1.60
IT	17.22	15.05	35.13	46.38	0.00	1.91	5.04	0.68
CA	126.13	4.41	1.83	2.75	1.38	0.00	11.38	0.22
JA	106.39	12.36	6.93	24.53	3.69	7.44	0.00	0.83
AR	2.09	0.18	0.27	1.06	0.61	0.14	0.62	0.00
BR	15.52	1.83	2.52	3.99	3.00	1.10	4.17	1.26
ME	22.63	0.70	0.51	0.82	0.09	0.95	0.49	0.16
TA	26.62	2.17	1.32	4.00	1.00	1.84	17.21	0.02
OP	30.83	2.58	6.09	5.90	10.01	1.15	28.59	0.06
UP	3.94	0.00	1.64	1.98	0.63	0.66	0.08	0.00
MP	8.30	0.13	0.35	0.00	0.09	0.15	1.50	0.00
OI	42.93	79.59	89.71	172.44	49.52	5.34	26.75	1.50
KS	61.99	9.70	4.33	13.31	2.92	4.05	36.01	0.18
OL	21.50	2.33	2.00	4.99	1.95	1.21	3.70	1.21
AN	9.64	4.87	9.44	8.12	7.70	0.54	7.54	0.12
RO	33.43	18.64	24.16	47.56	28.33	3.75	51.42	0.70
Totals								
Exports	582.39	227.43	278.89	499.81	215.90	182.38	370.27	15.30
Imports	617.69	251.61	287.53	440.83	211.73	164.14	293.76	11.83
Trade balance	−35.30	−24.18	−8.63	58.98	4.18	18.24	76.51	3.47

For an explanation of country abbreviations see table B-3.

				Importer				
BR	ME	TA	OP	OI	KS	OL	AN	RO
7.67	31.27	23.47	14.39	82.66	47.51	23.75	10.83	47.83
0.75	0.44	0.94	9.59	67.01	7.52	1.95	7.28	20.49
1.44	0.60	1.18	8.34	77.48	4.68	5.21	15.41	32.63
2.30	1.28	3.02	10.72	205.87	8.23	3.05	9.12	47.85
0.73	0.34	1.01	10.98	56.23	4.36	1.88	5.08	13.86
1.15	0.61	2.21	1.43	7.54	4.45	1.66	1.05	14.18
1.55	1.15	23.58	16.09	48.21	59.47	6.87	4.27	46.90
1.06	0.14	0.94	0.55	2.77	0.21	1.37	0.62	2.68
0.00	0.37	0.29	2.56	7.52	1.66	3.70	1.47	6.26
0.63	0.00	0.53	0.08	2.55	0.84	1.76	0.13	2.12
0.06	0.07	0.00	2.56	4.01	13.67	1.46	1.65	5.45
4.07	0.02	2.98	0.00	15.12	9.45	3.85	2.14	21.87
0.00	0.00	0.00	0.00	7.08	0.00	0.00	0.00	0.00
0.00	0.00	0.00	0.00	0.61	0.00	0.00	0.00	0.00
2.18	1.67	7.14	13.29	237.10	18.40	7.35	13.54	77.54
0.24	0.27	4.36	5.27	20.54	22.89	3.41	3.59	60.71
1.74	0.21	1.21	0.72	26.01	2.97	5.14	0.66	5.42
0.61	0.06	2.11	0.74	14.54	1.89	0.70	6.03	23.04
2.61	0.57	11.74	14.09	80.63	74.35	1.63	7.43	177.16
57.24	46.11	83.10	144.70	845.99	253.77	82.98	97.71	578.22
28.78	39.07	86.72	111.42	963.50	282.53	74.73	90.32	606.01
28.46	7.04	−3.62	33.28	−117.51	−28.76	8.24	7.39	−27.79

Other Publications from the Institute

POLICY ANALYSES IN INTERNATIONAL ECONOMICS SERIES

BOOKS

World Agricultural Trade: Building a Consensus
William M. Miner and Dale E. Hathaway, editors/1988

Japan in the World Economy
Bela Balassa and Marcus Noland/1988

America in the World Economy: A Strategy for the 1990s
C. Fred Bergsten/1988

SPECIAL REPORTS

FORTHCOMING

United States External Adjustment and the World Economy
William R. Cline

More Free Trade Areas?
Jeffrey J. Schott

Free Trade Areas and United States Trade Policy
Jeffrey J. Schott, editor

Foreign Direct Investment in the United States
Edward M. Graham and Paul R. Krugman

Equilibrium Exchange Rates: An Update
John Williamson

Oil Crisis Intervention: A Blueprint for International Cooperation
Philip K. Verleger, Jr.

Exchange Rate Policy Making in the United States
I. M. Destler and C. Randall Henning

The Debt of Low-Income Africa: Issues and Options for the United States
Carol Lancaster